Kenzo Tange

Kenzo Tange
by Robin Boyd

George Braziller   New York   1962

Library of Congress Catalog Card Number: 62–16267

Printed in the United States of America

First Printing

"Creation in Present-day Architecture
and the Japanese Tradition" by Kenzo Tange
is reprinted in abridged form
from the magazine SHINKENCHIKU (The Japan Architect)
June, 1956, with the kind permission
of the author and the publishers.

Contents

A decade after the war in the Pacific ended, the Western
world gradually began to realize that many important qualities of its accepted modern architecture were in fact very old.
These qualities had existed for centuries in many Japanese
buildings. Japanese tradition contained not only the simplicity, lightness, and openness which contemporary Western
designers had recently been advocating, not only the modu-
lated repetition of elements so familiar in contemporary
Western building, but it often demonstrated the same aesthetic
values as well. It relied on the use of ingenuous construction
and untreated natural materials to build a sort of refined extension of nature: a concentration of nature's own kind of
beauty.

Thus Japan was rediscovered. European and American
home magazines were enthusiastic over the shoji screen, bamboo, and colorless finishes—a new fashion trend was created.
More serious architects and critics began to examine with
curiosity and expectation the work of contemporary Japanese
designers. It became apparent that there were three or four
men of the highest standards and one or two who might be
considered as belonging to the ranks of the world's leaders.

One building in particular stood out from the early post-
war Japanese architecture. It was the Peace Museum at Hiroshima, a long, strong pavilion that looked entirely modern
and yet had a curiously evocative Japanese touch. Apprecia-
tion of the dignity and confidence of this work, allied perhaps
to a guilt complex that was readily stirred by the name Hiroshima, elevated this building to world prominence and its
architect, Kenzo Tange, to recognition as a full member in
the company of great contemporary architects. Commemorat-
ing the most momentous and disastrous innovation in human
history, the Peace Memorial Museum (plates 1, 3–5), the
design of which won a competition in 1949, is an astonish-
ingly mature work for what is actually the architect's first
building.

The hall is a long narrow structure, only one tall story high,
but elevated some twenty feet above the ground on recessed
concrete pillars, or *pilotis* (plates 1–5). The visitor mounts a
central hanging stairway (plate 3) to gain admittance to the
permanent exhibition. Showing the effects of the Hiroshima
bombing by means of an exhibition of photographs, models,
twisted relics, and plaster dummies of charred bodies, the
display finally turns to thoughts and hopes for peace. Was
ever the expressive side of the art of architecture faced with
a greater challenge? The task for Tange was to build a func-
tioning building, not a piece of sculpture, yet a building which

10   could not remain aloof from the emotional stresses inherent in the scheme. As a background to the displays' awful mixture of horror and hope, any kind of aestheticism, any attempt at a personal artistic gambol, would have been intolerably out of key.

The exhibits themselves are arranged and maintained in a way to be expected in a Japanese public building: as crudely as can be, with the coarsely lettered paper legends now yellowing and peeling. Yet, for once, the primitive coarseness of such public presentation is not disturbing. At least it errs in the right direction, for any evidence of self-conscious typography would have been much more offensive.

In a cultivated way, Tange's architecture also errs, if at all, in the direction of anonymity. Like the display technique, it is never obtrusive and hardly ever self-conscious. However, unlike the display technique, it has built these qualities deliberately. There are no apparent accidents and very few irrelevancies. The stripped concrete is of the correct degree of roughness. It is all as strong and unvacillating as anybody could want, but it does not show the exaggerated super-strength of later Japanese work. The form has just enough irregularity to avoid both monotony and any suspicion of lack of serious purpose. For instance, the vertical fins which make up the long walls on front and back, carrying sunshades between them on the south, are rhythmically spaced except at structural-bay divisions where they effectively miss a half-beat. It is, in short, a building in repose, without being asleep; a building of fitting dignity and solemnity. It could so easily have been more than that; many architects would have made more of it. But thanks to Tange's sensitivity its message is not weakened by any hint of overstatement.

The Museum stands in an open park, flanked by sympathetic Community Center and Hotel buildings (plates 2, 6–11). Although all three were planned by Tange, only the Museum was executed by him. On the axial approach line, some distance to the north, at the zero point of the bomb's blast, Tange also designed the Memorial to the Dead (plate 7). Here, the architect was not quite so confident of his ground, for this *is* sculpture. Tange has designed it as a heavy vault or hood of concrete, looking curiously like a saddle or a covered wagon, sheltering a block within which the known victims' names are inscribed. The hood was loosely based on a traditional form, the roof of the prehistoric *haniwa* house. Nevertheless, it is in the dangerously fashionable saddle shape, and it gives more than a hint of having been designed, contrived, by an architect. It does not look quite as inevitable, anonymous, and impersonal as one would wish.

The scale of the emotions in this Peace Park at Hiroshima

is, to use Tange's own hyphenated word, mass-human; it is
bigger than the personal, the individual human being. One
can but weep, or pray, for all humanity after contemplating
the terrible record and the small hopes recorded in the Museum. Tange's saddle vault is not, of course, in any way offensive; it simply fails to reach the dynamic balance which no
doubt he sought. It errs slightly on the side of private, personal sentiment.

All Tange's training was acquired in Imperial Japan before
the war ended and all his practice has been carried on in the
New Japan which followed. He was born in September, 1913,
too late to know much about the First World War and early
enough to have his preliminary architectural education completed before the second one began. In 1935, at the age of
twenty-two, he began studying in the Department of Architecture at Tokyo University. The promise of his work was offi-
cially recognized on graduation in 1938 when he was awarded
the *Tatsuno* prize for graduates. Between 1942 and 1945, he
took the Graduate Course in Architecture at Tokyo University, with some part-time work for the Tokyo planning authority on the side. He established a private practice after
the war by winning the 1949 open competition held for the
Hiroshima memorial project. After that, his name was established and work of a similar kind—convention halls, city
halls, libraries, memorial halls—kept him fully occupied.
At the same time, he accepted a professorship at Tokyo
University. While never deviating from the object of being
primarily a builder and not a teacher, he managed for some
years to divide his activities between lecture room and office.
As the creative work mounted, however, so did the pressures,
and he moved his practice to the University. Meanwhile, he
had built up an ardent following of graduates and, somewhat
in the style of Walter Gropius whom he greatly admires, he
formed a group known as Kenzo Tange and His Team. The
team includes at present about twenty other architects and,
each year, it is supplemented by a few new graduates—re-
placements for older members of the team who drift into their
own practices. The team closely follows the Gropius working
methods, pooling ideas in self-searching discussion.
Since the Peace Museum project, Kenzo Tange's reputation
has been consolidated by many other excellent buildings,
and he has received formal recognition on a number of occasions. Three times he has accepted the highly respected
Annual Prize of the Architectural Institute of Japan. In 1957,
he was invited to São Paulo to sit on the jury awarding
international prizes at the Bienale. In 1958 he visited Hawaii

12   to receive the Pan-Pacific Citation, and in 1959 the Paris magazine *L'Architecture d'Aujourd'hui* awarded him its *Prix Internationale*. During the academic year 1959–60, Tange accepted a post as visiting professor at the Massachusetts Institute of Technology.[1]

Tange is an engagingly modest man who does not imagine himself as a leading form-giver. He sees himself and his work in a state of transition, belonging in a nation and a world that are still involved in the later stages of the industrial revolution. The most he expects to be able to do is create a dynamic balance between the inconsistencies which worry him, the inconsistencies which must worry any sensitive man attempting to build well in the modern world.

Although Tange is Japanese, he is also an architect of the world. To him, the Parthenon and the medieval cathedrals are as much a part of architectural tradition as the Katsura Palace and the Ise Shrines. Yet he is also a regionalist, believing that a building in Tokyo should be different from one in Los Angeles, not for the sake of being Japanese, but because Tokyo and Los Angeles are different in background and living habits. The Pacific wind which blows on each blows in different directions, and Tange feels that even concrete should be tempered by this fact. Any building material must be affected, automatically, if the architect designs appropriately and realistically for each occasion.

When Tange works in concrete, as he usually does, his buildings reflect Le Corbusier's way of handling this material. But he has demonstrated that he can use other materials with great individuality and originality. His buildings vary greatly in form and character. His admirers praise this as a reflection of his aim to express the particular reality of each building. His critics, on the other hand, point to it as evidence that he is still rather eclectic and has developed no clear style of his own. Tange himself, as his own most studious critic, takes the latter view. Although it may be true that he has not yet developed a fixed, personal visual style, it is equally true that some of his latest buildings carry an unmistakable signature. If the visual character varies to suit each task in hand, his intellectual approach to the problem of building in general remains consistent. It is to find the vital balance which expresses the reality of each building problem and simultaneously to create a valid architectural image for modern Japan.

The occasional flavor of tradition in Tange's buildings is a product of this approach. He is an authority on Japanese traditions who knows and respects the traditional forms enough to want to avoid counterfeiting them.[2] The touch of tradition in his work is often elusive because what he wants to follow is the best traditional method, not the result. He seems to stand halfway between the conventional traditionalists and a slightly older man like Kunio Mayekawa, who is much more extroverted, perhaps more brilliantly creative, certainly more extravagant. The comparison between these two men is made with every wish to avoid any suggestion of competition, and simply in an attempt to relate the two, who are about equally representative of the new architecture of Japan. Tange is better known abroad, and more widely and better appreciated by the Japanese public—but not always by the intellectuals.[3]

To a Western viewer, the big question of modern Japanese design is whether certain qualities of traditional Japanese architecture have been retained, developed, or neglected by contemporary architects. In rural Japan, clear of the litter of Japanese cities, the regional traditions still live on, barely disturbed. They are found, most obviously, in the preserved shrines and temples, detached and insulated from the 20th century by the raked gravel or the stones and moss of their Zen gardens. The old serenity is not confined to these withdrawn displays, however, for the humble country cottage, hemmed in by its tightly cultivated green paddy, is made in one of the world's most attractive peasant vernaculars. The grays of its untreated wood and bronzed tiles or thatched roof have a rare serenity and distinctive charm. A village of cottages, all made with precisely the same materials and technique but with functional variations in shape, may be accidental and formless, but it is always harmonious within itself and within the landscape.

Buildings, however, are not always the most important part of this tradition. Often the more impressive qualities are in the semi-confined open-air spaces between them; spaces which usually have been planned with the same care and skill as the forms. The main fascination here is quite apart from the gardening, that formal concentration of natural beauty. It is also quite apart from the constant delights of the color, the warm grays of thatch and bare timber merging with white stones, green leaves, and water. The important thing is the space itself. The open-pavilion form, with the separate surrounding fence which acts almost as a detached wall, provides feelings of spacious semi-enclosure—an easy blending of indoors and outdoors—and fascinating visual effects of the half-revealed, always coaxing the viewer to look through or beyond another building. These are all qualities of spatial design only recently discovered in the West and of enormous interest to Western architects and critics.

There are many personal ways of supporting tradition. In the Shin Kabuki Theater for traditional drama in Osaka, for example, Togo Murano has made a multi-story concrete building reflect the pagoda-like repetitive curves of the nearby

14 16th-century Osaka Castle. This is not Tange's method. Tange, one can only repeat, wants to be, and usually is, a realist in the most reputable meaning of that word. He does not work, or play, with tradition. It is something which he has absorbed, something which he deeply respects and has loved. But it also awes him and almost repels him because of the suffocating influence it could have on his own creative activities. Consequently, the ancient qualities appear in his work almost inadvertently. One would hardly expect them to be apparent when he designs an advertising office in the middle of Osaka, and they are not. But in more fertile conditions, such as the Art Center of Tokyo's Sogetsu, even though the restrictions of a modern city site are all but enough to crush any spirit of serenity, the tradition comes through, easily and unconsciously translated.

Tange is continually writing. He claims not to enjoy it, but he feels compelled at every new turn to explain his artistic aims and ideals in black and white. Clearly he does this for his own benefit as much as for anyone else's. His explanations usually reflect nothing more than the search for truth, and for him this is the problem of how to seek out and express "the realities" of the human occupation and the structure of a building. Specifically, it is a question of how, in Tange's words, "to give an image to the unawakened desires of society." Why should Tange, or any architect, feel this need to define his duties in society? Tange feels the need because to him the social implications of all buildings, their great, if usually subconscious, influence on people's lives, pose the most important and fascinating problems of his art. To ignore these problems is to reduce architecture to a purely aesthetic task, the object being to create something pleasing to the eyes of those people one wants to please; in other words, to create beauty—a relative, visual beauty with no ultimate meaning.

Like every other serious architect, Tange is sometimes pulled in two directions: toward what his reasoning tells him is the reality of the building, and toward the games that his trained imagination would like to play. This fundamental built-in conflict of the architectural art—reality versus the visual ideal—is the basis of most theoretical architectural writing. It is an unresolved conflict which begs for solution, attracting critics in the same way that the problem of perpetual motion attracted inventors. It is a basic inconsistency of the art; and Tange, who encourages his own awareness of inconsistencies, is vitally conscious of his own need to define where he stands in the conflict.

At the beginning of his creative life, just after the war, he stood most clearly on the side of reality, and held a virtually anti-aesthetic attitude. Now, as his personal creative imagination gains freedom and sharpness by solving each new and ever-more-exacting problem, he seems to recognize the enticements of aestheticism; but there is no question of his surrendering to them. The fact that there is a conflict merely serves to sharpen his wits. "Inconsistency itself breeds vitality," he says, and this is a minor article of his philosophy.

The greatest, overriding inconsistency is the one "that arises from the confrontation of technology and human existence," he said in 1959. He has since put the same thought in many other ways. "We live in a world where great incompatibles coexist: the human scale and the superhuman scale, stability and mobility, permanence and change, identity and anonymity, comprehensibility and universality. These are the reflections of the gap between advancing technology and humanity as historical existence."[4] As a teacher he says, "It is a problem of technology versus humanity, and the task of today's architects and city planners is to build a bridge between these two things."[5] And as an optimistic observer he adds, "I like to think that there is something deep in our own world of reality that will create a dynamic balance between technology and human existence, the relationship between which has a decisive effect on contemporary cultural forms and social structure."[6]

The second pair of "great incompatibles" is tradition and creativity. It should be clear what is meant by these, although both terms are actually rather inadequate, especially the second. The opposite of tradition should take into account, as well as constructive thinking, the involuntary condition of being alive in the 20th century, of being aware of change, progress, and new values. In this conflict Tange stands on the side of creativity. "I do not believe that tradition as such can either be preserved or converted into creative drive," he has said. "If the smell of tradition is noticeable in my works . . . it is because our creative abilities have not flowered, because we are still in the transition toward creativity. I have no desire whatever to have my works appear traditional."[7] Another time, noting with a sense of resignation the unpremeditated resemblance of his Kurashiki City Hall to the old Japanese log-cabin-style warehouses, he observed, "We are still in the process of crystallization."

A third pair of "great incompatibles" is the anonymity and super-scale of the modern community opposing the wish and need of the individual for identification. "People are becoming more alike throughout the world," Tange said at the significant World Design Conference in Tokyo, in May, 1960. "They are being organized into huge groups in which they

16 become anonymous. The desire for individuality, however, seems to be basic to human nature. . . . An attempt at identity through advertising of one sort or another is evident, but by now the advertising is so disorderly that it too has become anonymous."

There are other incompatible elements in modern life and design which Tange has observed. Most of these, however, relate to the plain fact that the nature of individual man is in danger of becoming incompatible with the nature of man as he would be molded by technology and super-scale organization.

If Tange has forcefully pointed up in his writings these fundamental inconsistencies, this is perhaps not a surprising result of his native environment. The incompatibles and inconsistencies of which he speaks are international, but nowhere else are they so obtrusive as in Tokyo. This city, his city, is living, teeming evidence of all the problems, incongruities and incompatibles toward which practically all big modern communities seem to be headed. As Tange says, "Almost every district of Tokyo has approximately the same population density and buildings of the same height. They are all similar in function, and they are all growing in the same shoddy way. There is practically nothing to distinguish one place from another."[8] Tokyo is not only a perfect example of the supranational conflicts between individuality and universality, human and superhuman scale, tradition and progress, technology and humanity; but all of these international conditions are highlighted here by an additional and piquant conflict: Eastern versus Western cultures.

Now, it may be that no conflicts are involved, in a country which has accepted the cultural invasion by the West, when a Japanese girl sings, "I'm a Fujiyama Mamma." Perhaps this sort of thing is just a symptom of the Hollywood–*Life International* syndrome, and has nothing to do with the fact that some Japanese girls yearn to be what they cannot be. But there is at least a suggestion of submerged conflict in the consistency of the European image that is presented by the Japanese glamour industry. For instance, every shop fashion dummy is blonde; almost all really fashionable girls who can afford it have their eyes surgically altered; and every doll in the department store stares at the Japanese child with round blue eyes in a blond head. Something must build up inside a Japanese woman or child constantly confronted by these images.

Western ways have brought to Japanese cities, along with democracy and rising living standards for many people, all the mad visual trivia of our last sixty years. The architectural conflict is not simply traditional versus creative-modern. As

in the West, neither of these elements is at all obtrusive. The
center of the stage has been taken by the false-nosed come-
dians of the various fashions which have passed by since
Japan turned westward in the Meiji Era.

As rebuilt since the war, Tokyo has more than the average
share of presentable new buildings. But, since it also has an
extraordinary number of buildings, old and new, it displays
many examples that match the worst that any Western city
can contribute to the architectural comedy. Pompous neo-
classic Roman columns and friezes, looking never more ridic-
ulous, solemnify the facades of the larger banks. From a
slightly later date, the theaters display multitudinous parallel
lines rushing around streamlined corners. Here and there a
bit of Chicago *Tribune* Gothic appears. The current building
boom is represented by all the restless diagonals, the zigzag
silhouettes, the parodies of Edward Stone's grillwork and
Mies van der Rohe's gridwork, the meaningless decorative
trifles—even down to that classic symbol for a symbol in this
empty mid-century: three fish, one above the other—all the
gigantic trivia, the gewgaws and the gimmicks, all the visual
idiocy of the 20th century. It is reproduced tirelessly and ex-
cellently; it is bundled up in more than the usual amount of
tangled overhead wires; and it is illuminated by night in a
blaze of neon, explosions of color around Japanese characters
done in square-block style: a mad gnome's fairyland almost
surpassing Times Square in brilliance.

Obviously, Tange is appalled by this terrible mess of Tokyo,
this parody of both cultures. No architect single-handed can
do much about it, but he can contribute, along with all other
creative people in the community, to the development of a
more genuine popular culture expressing some of the realities
of their regional way of living. When "the smell of tradition"
enters Tange's work in the involuntary sort of way that it has
a habit of doing, he is probably contributing more than he
realizes. On the other hand, when he allows the Le Corbusier
influence to dominate too strongly, he is not notably assisting
Japan to find its own popular branch culture in the modern
world. Perhaps Tange's most vital contribution at the present
time is his relentless eloquence in stressing the need for designers, architects, and planners to cultivate a sense of reality rather than irresponsible beauty. To this end, he makes it
clear that he would be willing to forego beauty altogether if
he could not have a beauty with meaning and integrity.

In practice, how does Tange set out to find the point of
truth, or reality, between the popular and the creative sides
of the cultural gulf? Asking the question again in his own
words used at the 1960 World Design Conference in Tokyo—
"How can the gulf be spanned? How can order be imposed

on confusion?"—he answers this key problem of his architectural life in two ways.

The first is theoretical: human ingenuity, which can be stimulated by these very inconsistencies. The architect and the city planner, he says, are in a position to accept, and must accept, a responsibility to give visual and physical form to the vitality which resides dormant in the inconsistent community. He says, "I like to call this position 'vitalism'—I think of it as an organic life which includes order and freedom, mobility and stability." In this task of giving form to the mass vitality, "the role played by tradition is that of the catalyst, which encourages and stimulates a chemical reaction, but does not remain in the resulting compound. Thus, tradition can play a part in creation, but it does not of itself create."

The second answer is technological: as tradition is just a catalyst, so, to an extent, is technology. "To grasp the phenomenal aspects of things that are beginning or progressing and to accept these as order, or as the order given to us, is not realistic," he says. The function of the architect, the giving of the image to real life, is fulfilled only when created form, or order, enters. "Reality is a movement which includes inconsistencies. To discover order within these inconsistencies and to give form to this order is our task."

Some good architects, of course, are not impressed by theory. Others, although inspired, fail to convince us when they translate theories of truth into buildings. The test of Tange in his chosen field, which very decidedly is neither theorizing nor teaching, is not whether his philosophy and theories are good, but how well he transposes his search for truth and reality into building. One of his great concerns is the need for a methodology of design for contemporary architecture. While it is indisputable, he admits, that "simple defiance of methods taught by tradition is not realistic, nevertheless, new methods must be found by bringing architecture face to face with today's reality." In his own work his method seems to include six principal rules.

First, *simplicity of plan and form.* This is the basic formal rule; for the presentation of a complicated truth can be like saying that all the plays of Shaw are to be found in the dictionary.

The second rule is *typification,* which is Tange's word to describe his attitude to the functional content of architecture. The direct expressions of early functionalism he calls naïve. Instead, he attempts to draw out "the essential and progressive" elements which typify the function—or, perhaps, to interpret the function artistically before allowing form to

follow it. This rule explains his justification of such functional
anomalies as the vast empty entrance hall and the adjacent small crowded offices in the Kurashiki City Hall. "Typification," he says, "is the basic method of creation in architecture."

Strength is his third rule, for he wants architecture to insist. He rejects the elegance of Japanese tradition as weakness. In his own work, this rule certainly is evidenced by some extraordinarily strong and emphatic effects.

His fourth rule accepts a part of the Japanese tradition which was also enthusiastically adopted by modern Western architecture: a *ban on ornament*. As originally defined by Adolf Loos some sixty years ago, this ban was total. Lately it has been relaxed a little to allow meaningful ornament. Of course, what is meaningful to the designer may mean nothing to others; but that is the occupational hazard. However, certain ornaments are meaningful to most people; for example, a spring flower after a long winter. That is almost the only sort of ornament which has always been permitted in the Japanese interior, and it is the sort that Tange permits himself on occasion, even though the meaning is sometimes lost to a Western observer.

Allied to this rule is perhaps the most obvious one of all those required in the search for truth. It is the rule of *honesty to the materials* which one selects. Again, this fundamental principle is part of the Japanese tradition. It was lost in the West for centuries, but has been rediscovered by the 20th-century movement. It means never forcing material to work against its nature, and covering no material with some foreign matter for a purely visual effect. Hence the characteristic naked look of Tange's work, even more pronounced than it is in the rest of modern Japanese building. He carried it as far as leaving reconstructed-timber hardboard sheets raw in Tokyo City Hall partitions, and in showing the mechanical services above a light louvered ceiling in the Rikkyo University Library.

Finally, and perhaps most important, is the rule of avoiding at all costs the attitude of *fūryū*. *Fūryū* is the Japanese word that can be translated as "floating with the wind," or as "tasteful"—but in the sense that it is tasteful not to notice unpleasant realities. Perhaps it is best translated as "kidding yourself." Tange explains it thus, "One is reminded of the common practice of hanging a little bamboo cage containing insects in one's garden during the summer. In the evening, when one hears the song of the insects, one thinks, 'Ah, how cool it is!' One does not, however, nullify the heat; one simply escapes it by self-deception." Tange makes much of this, and

20 some of his most impassioned and effective writing is devoted to the subject.

Furyu is an antirealist, anti-action element in Japanese life, fostered no doubt by age-old ingrown poverty and frustration, which Tange wants to shake out of the national psyche. It is allied to the concept of *mono-no-aware*, or the understanding of the beauty and pathos of man and nature. It was encouraged by Zen Buddhism, with its self-emptying, self-denying attitude toward creation. *Furyu* was, and is, a compromise which made it possible to live with bitterly uncomfortable reality.

Kenzo Tange knows very well, however, that *furyu* is just what Europeans find so fascinating about Japan. It is at the heart of nine tenths of the West's fashionable counterfeiting of a Japanese style: "Japonica," or "Shibui," as it is called with more or less irony. *Furyu* is responsible for the elegant prettiness that still runs through so much of the withdrawn, private, indoor side of Japanese life. It entails a perfectionist's concentration on detail, typified by the delicately designed and beautifully colored matchboxes of modern Japan. "Meaningless prettiness," says Tange, and he adds with a self-deprecating laugh, "I hate it."

The theme of Tange's book on the Katsura Palace is the interaction of two conflicting elements in Japanese architectural history. The palace, he says, belongs basically to one branch, which stems from the aristocratic culture of the ancient imperial court. This is what the West knows best as "Japanese." "I see in it something of *Yoyoi* culture," writes Tange, "a definite, formal aesthetic; quiet, well-balanced and dominated by a subjective, lyrical frame of mind." But another force is present, "the vital culture-forming energy" of the Japanese masses, which clashes with the formal aristocratic aesthetic. "I think of this as the *Jōmon* principle," says Tange "—the primitive life force of the Japanese race."

Yoyoi and *Jōmon* are still conflicting elements in Japanese life, and their interaction does not always result in a beauty as of Katsura. Translating these terms into modern conditions and English, they could possibly be called respectively repose and force, or delicacy and coarseness, or tenderness and callousness, and as such they constitute for many Western visitors the most puzzling pair of all the inconsistencies in modern Japan. The former quality in these pairs, the *Yoyoi*, is mostly feminine and usually found only indoors. The latter, the *Jomon*, is masculine and found mostly in the public street.

Whatever one calls these elements, their separate identities impinge continuously on the Westerner, who comes from a culture in which similar pairs of elements are much more homogenized, or are at least separated on a class or social basis, not on a gender basis in all levels of society. Thus, the

Westerner finds much geisha sweetness on the surface of
Japan, yet he glimpses another side. He sees this, for instance,
in the callousness which is normally displayed toward any victims of accidents, from an individual traffic casualty to the
masses afflicted by some national disaster like an earthquake
or a flood. In these cases the phenomenon of *jiko*, or stranger-
death, applies, and leaves the individual observer unaffected
by the suffering.

The Westerner finds *jiko* of the city everywhere: rubbish, untidiness, breakage, lack of hygiene, lack of maintenance, lack
of civic responsibility in practically every public place, including public buildings. In the long view, a modern Japanese
town presents through the smog a view of unholy litter, of
stained and chipped concrete, and gaudy neon signs on rusted
steel scaffolds. Yet the close view reveals many thoughtful,
creative, beautiful buildings by men like Tange, Mayekawa,
Murata, Maki, and others—more architects of real quality
per new building than in most countries. And in the closest
view there is the impeccable order and cleanliness to be found
as soon as one's slippers touch *tatami*, the interior floor
mats.

Beauty to the Japanese is a personal and secret thing. The
Westerner, if he pauses to think, must agree with that. But
he still may ask if it need be so withdrawn and so private
and so insulated from the outdoor reality. Somehow Western
civilization has succeeded by now in blending callousness and
consideration, selfishness and public spirit, the outdoor and
the indoor personality, to such an extent that neither shows in
isolation very often. The West keeps its shoes on indoors.
The Japanese tea ceremony, the flower arrangements, the
geishas, the graciousness of most social intercourse, all suggest a culture infinitely more refined than that of the West.
It is largely a feminine culture, however; and Japan, despite
radical reforms since the war, is still a country where it is
more comfortable if you can arrange in advance to be male.

This aesthetic division is a vital consideration for a Japanese architect and somehow has always been apparent in building. The history of Japanese architecture is notably different
from that of the West; because there have been no great stylis-
tic changes, no violent breaks in the evolution, no dead pas-
sages and sudden renaissances. Consistently, through many
centuries, there have been two distinctly different approaches
to construction. One, exemplified by the shrine and temple
built of huge forest logs, is heavy and over-strong for the
job to be done; it is solid and permanent. The other, exemplified by the teahouse with softly sliding paper doors and
trembling bamboos in ceiling and screens, is delicate and

22 barely sufficient for the task. These two are ever present: the forceful and the frail; the masculine and the feminine.

Western architecture characteristically has never conspicuously separated into genders. Nevertheless, there has been a feminine tendency in recent commercial building, with its over-precious lightness and delicacy of glass and polished metal. In reaction to this, a new movement began in Europe some ten years ago with the avowed intent of returning to the fundamentals of building. It reveled in such things as rough concrete and exposed pipes, and it soon came to be called the New Brutalism. It so happened that at about the same time the great Le Corbusier in France began to expand his earlier tendencies toward more than adequate strength in design and more than normal coarseness in the finishing of his raw concrete. The New Brutalists and Le Corbusier really are not related, but the two images they present are inclined to get confused and identified with each other. Anywhere in the world, rough and heavy concrete work is likely to be called Brutalist or Corbu-style, or both. It is inevitable that Japan has many new buildings which could be so described for it has decisively chosen the masculine gender of modern architecture.

The Japanese earthquake hazard practically rules out brick as a structure and glass as a wall. Steel is expensive. Stone is scarce. Concrete is the natural material for construction of everything bigger than a house; and stripped concrete, patterned by the grain and knots of the wood of its formwork, is the natural surface texture. Both are used by adventurous expressionists like Mayekawa as well as by quite commercial designers of ordinary office blocks. Sometimes, as in the richer office blocks of Marunouchi, the concrete is overlaid with expensive materials, but still it is always allowed to show somewhere: a sort of rich man's Brutalism.

For the great majority of creative Japanese architects then, Corbu-style concrete is an idiom which overrules all other modern influences at work. This is not a new development. Japan has always thought of modern architecture as a European movement, despite the fact that her first direct contact was with Frank Lloyd Wright.[9] Through the late 1920's, Japanese architects heard more about the movement that was rising in Europe: Gropius and the Bauhaus, and Le Corbusier. In 1927 Torao Saito translated sections of Le Corbusier's rousing manifesto, *L'Esprit Nouveau,* into Japanese. Later, his *Vers Une Architecture* was also translated. Kunio Mayekawa was one of several young Japanese architects who visited Europe to study, and he actually worked with Le Corbusier. Meanwhile Antonin Raymond, a Czech-American who had come to Tokyo with Wright and remained there, was

building the first concrete buildings in Japan which reflected
the modern European theories. After the Second World War, when Tange began practice, Japanese architects looked again to Europe for inspiration in design, and to the United States mainly for instruction in techniques. In 1959 Japan's long but distant relationship with Le Corbusier was finally cemented in the building of the National Museum of Western Art in Tokyo, to the master's own idiomatic design.

The European-concrete-Corbu idiom is the one which Tange, with rare exceptions, has adopted. He accepts it as part of the modern background of Japan. He is an individualist who is developing a style, but it is a style within this idiom which was largely crystallized about the time that he completed his training. This is no criticism, for Tange is pleased to claim that his work is very close in spirit to that of several of his leading confreres and, furthermore, that he would rather contribute to a broad order than develop an individual idiom.

It would be wrong to suggest Japanese submissiveness in this relationship. Although it is true that for many years Japan was virtually an architectural colony of Europe, this changed in 1960 when the Japanese called a World Design Conference in Tokyo—tantamount to a declaration of independence. After that conference, modern Japanese architecture was well established in the world scene and, incidentally, Kenzo Tange, by his distinguished part in the conference, was confirmed in his position as the West's favorite Japanese architect. Although established in its own right, Japanese modern architecture still admits to being decisively influenced by the West; while the West, of course, admits with equal humility to the influence of Japanese traditions.

Although much Japanese work can be, and has been, described as Brutalist, this term (which was always an ironic word) is not really appropriate. The modern Japanese architectural brute is relatively tame. Tange sees it simply as an expression in modern terms of the stronger parent in Japanese tradition. It is certainly strong, and defiantly masculine. In fact the brute sometimes appears to be over-strong and over-masculine, to the extent that the sensitive and feminine side is entirely overwhelmed. Building is surely no closer to the truth, to the ultimate balance, if it falls over backward in retreat from the weak prettiness of fashion. Almost certainly the exaggerations in a great deal of this work will appear clumsy rather than strong in a few years, and then some other sort of reaction will set in, but the mood of Japanese architects is such that there could be no relapse into *furyu*.

How does Tange, with his keen sensibility to the need for a dynamic and genuine balance between inconsistencies, con-

24   trol this potentially dangerous use of coarse concrete? Like
many other architects, he does not hesitate to use more concrete than is necessary for a job. An examination of his buildings, or their illustrations in these pages, reveals a few in-
stances of super-redundancy in the design of elements such
as handrails and roof edge-beams, apparently done simply
for architectural effect. The visual result is certainly impressive, adding to the firmness of the statement he desires to
make. It is also a fairly satisfying link with the masculine
branch of Japanese tradition. At times, however, the work appears over-strong—dangerous to the extent mentioned: that it
may look affected after a short time, when the enticements
of the visual effect fade with familiarity.

Examples of this sort of potential clumsiness are not frequent in Tange's work—not nearly as frequent, I think it
fair to say, as in the work of his distinguished contempo-
raries. Nonetheless, the danger is there, and Tange is certainly aware of it. Yet by his architectural nature, he would
rather risk being over-strong than appear in any way in-
decisive or weak. Moreover, he does not drag the idiom
blindly into conditions where it would not be appropriate.
His practice has developed by chance into a fairly narrow
field of medium-sized buildings, mainly public buildings, for
which the idiom is naturally suited. He has not designed
residences, except for his own house, and in this house he
did not make use of the coarse concrete idiom. This exercise
in homely materials is not weaker than the heavy monuments
he has built for public use. It is, however, much milder, and
proves he can work successfully on an intimate scale.

Yet Tange is by no means a *tatami*, domestic-retreat, architect; he is of the world. And what the rest of the world wants
to know is whether he, in the realities of everyday building,
can achieve the balance he seeks, between the serenity of
centuries of experience and a restless modern creative urge.

Tange's career as an architect may be divided without excessive oversimplification into four phases, which are, of course, linked by his private attitudes and disciplines and merge into one another. When he first opened private practice in Tokyo and began his postponed career in building he was thirty-seven, which meant he was young enough to want to experiment and old enough to be respectful of experience. Thus, in the early years two phases alternated. In one phase, conventional rectangular forms and conservative structural frames were impeccably planned with precocious poise and developed a detached sense of repose. The smell of tradition is most noticeable in this phase, which includes the Hiroshima Peace Museum, Tokyo City Hall, and Tange's own home.

In the second, but simultaneous, style of his work, Tange became a prominent member of the international avant-garde of the time, alert to all the potential excitement of shell concrete, plastic form, and advanced geometry. Early trophies of his adventures in this phase are the Children's Library at Hiroshima, designed in his first year of practice, and the Ehime Convention Center of a year later. This phase soon passed, although as late as 1955 he designed the Shizuoka Convention Hall, the best example of all with its warped-plane roof.

However, even while his interest in plastic shapes faded, the emphasis on structure which marked these experiments was passed on and absorbed into his more restful rectilinear forms, to produce the third Tange phase. This could be called his *trabeated* phase: his beam period. Super-heavy beams of concrete are square cut, articulated, crossed and projected like giant lumber planks. Most of his buildings between 1955 and 1960 glorified the concrete beam, nowhere more effectively than in the Kagawa office building at Takamatsu.

Tange's fourth and present phase is a logical extension of the last. The solid concrete structure is no longer merely accentuated in details like the main beams, the roof, and balustrades. It dominates completely so that massive concrete is the sole visible medium. Windows as such disappear, recessed somewhere behind horizontal slits between hefty planks. The building becomes all structure, with a primitive, almost elemental air, like a log cabin. The purest expression of this phase so far is the Kurashiki City Hall. Other projects now on the drawing board suggest that a fifth and even bolder phase will soon appear.

A detailed view of Tange's development, and of the particular achievement of individual buildings, is best gained through examination of his major works.

Designed and erected during the period when the Hiroshima project was under way, the Ehime Convention Center and the Hiroshima Children's Library represent the start of Tange's plastic phase. The Ehime Convention Center was designed in 1952 and completed in 1953 at Matsuyama, on the island of Shikoku. It consists of two halls, circular in plan, linked by an administration wing (plates 12–16). The larger hall has a shallow, domed roof of impressive span (165 feet), supported on its perimeter by sturdy concrete piers which also carry, lower down, the sloping floor of the auditorium, holding it above the ground. The smaller one is more ingenious and makes a perfect female companion for the robust auditorium. In this case the circular room was constructed by first erecting at the center something like the bell of a huge trumpet in concrete sprouting from the ground and opening to the sky. Around this, between the edge of the trumpet and the ground, Tange then formed a cylinder made of glass, with light steel vertical stiffening trusses on the outside. The administration wing which joins these two circular structures is flat roofed and unobtrusive.

A sister of the smaller structure appeared a year earlier in the Children's Library at Hiroshima (plate 17). This delicate little building stands in a stony park not far from the Peace Park. It was opened in 1952 and was the first Tange building to be completed. The basis of the design, the trumpet bell, was clearly an idea dominated by structural theory, yet its circular plan also worked well for the radial spokes of bookshelves with reading spaces between (plate 18). More important, the spatial quality seems to relate appropriately to the occupants. From inside the building the opposed curves of the concrete trumpet suggest a romantic, cavelike enclosure —but a cave pulled inside out, simultaneously sheltering and extroverted, never oppressive. From the outside the trumpet can be seen through the glass only by those curious enough to want to see what is supporting the roof of a building with walls so frail. When first completed it must have looked as light and gay as a paper lantern hanging in one of the surrounding trees.

This charming library was warmly received by the architectural press and was instrumental in earning Tange the award of the first Pan-Pacific Citation given by the architects of Hawaii. Yet today the building is in a sad state of disrepair and is apparently not utilized to capacity. Part of the responsibility for this rests with the architectural concept. Another part rests with the failure to anticipate the lack of reasonable care it would receive. But at least half the trouble is surely the unpredictable collapse of even minimal maintenance.

The building seems to have been misconceived to an extent which is familiar enough among architects' first works: its eyes were too big for its budget. The unscreened glass perimeter wall seems quite impractical for Hiroshima's fierce summer heat, without provision being made for either sunshading or powerful air conditioning, or both. It had neither. Those who have to work in it have slung casual and inadequate bamboo blinds inside the glass on the southwest segment. The lack of sun screening is the limit of the concept's responsibility for the failure, but the heat seems to have demoralized everyone. The limited budget obtrudes again in the use of wood for the opening doors and windows. These have never been repainted in the building's life; and as a consequence some windows appear to be permanently jammed shut while others are permanently stuck slightly open. None of this is necessary for with only a little mothering and money the building could still be restored. In the absence of any such care, glass is cracked and holed by baseballs: the building stands erect, but battered.

Largely because of its neglect, the Children's Library is, now, no longer a Tange success. Yet, it is still endearingly unsuccessful, because it was done with sympathy, imagination, and the best intentions. The early collapse of the unsubstantial details in this, his first completed building, was of great significance in Tange's development. Never again did he err on the side of lightness in his public buildings.

Tange designed his own home in the suburbs of Tokyo in 1951 and completed it in 1953 (plates 19–27), concurrently with his plastic concrete adventures at Matsuyama and Hiroshima. In his house he reverted to homely materials—wood, tiles, rice-paper screens—and he frankly took as starting point the traditional domestic idiom. However, he controlled the idiom with unequivocal 20th-century disciplines, and he retained his individuality and creativity within it. The form belongs to his first, reserved, rectilinear phase. The plan is, as always, a model of simplicity: a spacious, flexible living space wrapped right around a central utility core (plate 19).

This house is strong in its simplicity. Although it appears to be as light as air and lacks the massive concrete of his bigger, later works, it is not weak. Although its finishes are done with traditional, impeccable Japanese craftsmanship, it is not effete. The one deliberately rebellious touch is a slashed scribble of action-painting (plate 24) on a *fusuma*, or opaque sliding screen, in a corner of the living room. This

28 painting accentuates the precision of the remainder, and
perhaps that was why it was introduced. It also suggests a
rude desire to break the discipline, a compulsive defacement
of the disturbingly pretty things in the tradition. One can't
help thinking that such defacement, if really necessary, could
have been achieved more economically by occasionally re-
laxing the supervision of the painstaking work of the builders.

Nevertheless, in this artless-looking house it may be that
Tange has come closer to expressing a reality of modern
Japan than he has in most of his early monumental works.
He also seems to have achieved the dynamic balance between
the various inconsistencies that exercise his mind, chiefly the
one between tradition and creativity. The fact that this little
building is one of his most successful works gives it an im-
portance out of proportion to its size. It is his own home, and
an architect's home (whether he designed it for himself or
not) is surely the most revealing thing about him.

Tsuda College Library (plates 28–32), Shimizu City Hall
(plates 33–36), and the Toshoinsatsu Printing Plant at
Numazu (plates 37–38) were all designed in a busy year,
1953, early in Tange's practice, and were built the following year. They are transitional between his first, reserved
phase and the heavy trabeation of his later monumental work.
They are neat, light buildings, neither parsimonious nor redundant in the scale of their structural parts; they are un-
pretentious and convincing. .

An adventurous approach to structure appears again in
the third example, the printing plant. The roof of this big
square single-story factory is supported on a double row of
legs down the center, and it cantilevers out in a series of airplane-wing trusses, a hundred and thirty feet on each side.
The outer wing tips are tied down, rather than held up, by
steel stanchions. All this is expressed plainly on the outside,
where the central legs, the airplane-wing ends of the roof,
and the vertical steel ties at the ends all stand slightly forward,
clear of the front of the factory's flat glass wall.

The City Hall of Kurayoshi (plates 39–45) in the Tottori
Prefecture on the north of Honshu Island near the Sea of
Japan, and the Sumi Memorial Hall (plates 46–51) at Ichinomiya, a few miles north of Nagoya, are two fine, similar
buildings from the beginning of the third phase of Tange's
work. Both were designed in 1955. The former was built in
1956 and the latter the following year. At this time Tange's
confidence in handling concrete was growing rapidly. Super-
strength beams appeared for the first time in these two buildings. Often they project out beyond the wall at full thickness
to support, more than adequately, some quite light balcony
or roof. These beams are not tapered to the end, as was once

the common practice when reinforced concrete was shaped to
express the stresses within it. They remain full size to the
end, where they are cut off suddenly as if by a saw.

The handrails began to grow in these two buildings, and
in the central stairwell at Kurayoshi they reach the mammoth
proportions (about eighteen by fifteen inches) that were to
become familiar a year or two later (plate 42). The broad,
straight stairway that these Kurayoshi handrails protect is set
in a wide two-story foyer of elemental starkness. The floor is
plain concrete, the ceiling a giant comb of deep concrete
beams like fallen forest logs.

In contrast to this strength both buildings introduce a little
grillwork (plates 40, 41, 50): open concrete blocks laid
with staggered joints, a pretty touch of a kind that was soon
to be resolutely eradicated from Tange buildings.

On the other hand, in the Sumi Hall another source of
Tange's later and more powerful phase was shown clearly
for the first time (plate 46). This is *Le Style Corbu*. Sumi's
main front wall to the street, for example, is a long single-
story expanse of battered wall, blank on each side of a wide
central entrance gash, except for five rain spouts and four
little box-framed windows. These are all projected forward
sculpturally to exploit sun shadows. The whole has a strong
scent of the master.

The City Hall at Tokyo (plates 52–60), or rather the only
wing of it that has been built, was not completed until 1957;
but since it was designed in 1952, for an invited competition,
it represents the first phase of Tange's development. It is light
and it is restful. At the same time, it benefited from the experience of extra years of practice, so the statement is clearer
and more confident than before. It leads up to the abundant
strength shown at Takamatsu, but does not yet anticipate the
redundant strength later to be applied at Kurashiki.

If you prefer Tange's later work, his more aggressively
insistent buildings, this city hall is unexciting. In this central urban setting, reasonable decorum surely called for a
gray flannel suit, and this, with occasional informalities, is
what Tange properly gave it. This first part of a future complex is a long, ten-story block of offices circumscribed by all
the problems of light, access and economy which have been
responsible, all over the world, for countless hundreds of
bland, efficient filing cabinets for clerks.

Tange was not prepared to accept the apparent economic
rule that an office façade has to be flat, and therefore either
unconscionably dull or unacceptably decorated. With every
justification, considering the Tokyo summer, he extended a
grid of horizontal concrete sunshades and vertical metal sun
baffles beyond the glass face, forming an egg-crate, with

cells scaled roughly to the individual offices behind (plate 52). This is a neat suit for an office block, and it was as far as he was prepared to go in formalities. The external elements which sprout out of the surrounding pavement are attractively independent touches, like boutonnieres. The floodlights for the front of the building (plate 54) are especially piquant; their supports are solid trunks growing about five feet high out of the swirled granite cobblestones of the forecourt. They are like odd tentacles of the paving reaching up to caress the building with their beams.

The ground-floor foyer, as usual in Tange's public buildings, is two stories high. It is paved with the same rough granite cobblestone as used in the forecourt, except for polished marble paths set in flush on the lines of the busiest traffic (plate 58). As always in modern Japan there is no color in the natural materials of the structure, only a variety of grays. But vivid, indeed violent, color has been introduced in a number of low-relief ceramic murals by Taro Okamoto. To me these seem singularly unnecessary.

The Shizuoka Convention Hall (plates 61–68), now used as a public gymnasium and stadium in the provincial city of Shizuoka, was Tange's last obvious experiment in plastic structure. Although he is still interested in adventuring into strange shapes and systems, the structural theme that he adopts today is more integrated with the humanistic theme, minimizing the insistent cleverness of the structure. The Shizuoka Hall is out of place in the chronology of his work, having been designed in 1955, while its form belongs better in the 1952 period, alongside the positive and negative domes at Matsuyama.

The Convention Hall stands in the rather moth-eaten municipal Sumpu Park, with the nearest buildings almost out of sight behind banks of trees. No question of architectural etiquette was posed by visible structures, and the open site called for a self-centered monolithic form, which is what Tange gave it—with a flourish. He planned the hall as a square set diagonally to the approach road through the park, and he drew over it a roof which is a saddle in shape, but trimmed down to its geometrical elements. Sweeping in a two-way curve down to the corners at each side and up to a peak at front and back, it is a pure hyperbolic paraboloid. Introduced to building by the engineer-designers (notably Felix Candela and Matthew Novicki), the opposing curves of the saddle fascinated many architects of the international avant-garde, including Le Corbusier, for several years after 1953. It can be constructed by cables woven in tension, pulling against each other, or it can be made up of rigid, straight members set in a grid, but warped, as though the corners

were held between thumbs and forefingers of two giant hands
and then twisted. Either way the inherent strength of the
curves offers an economical way for a roof to span a large
area. Tange used the latter method. His roof is supported
on a twisted grid of small concrete beams.

The walls of the building below this twisted roof are made
in the heavyweight concrete idiom which Tange had adopted
by this time. Each wall is wedge shaped, rising from head-
height at the low ends up to some forty-five feet in front and
back. The two walls facing the approach are made up of a
series of concrete fins with recessed, glazed panels between
them (plates 61, 68). The other two walls are blind, but zig-
zagged in plan for strength and for internal acoustic reasons
(plate 62). The heavy concrete edge-beams of the roof also
taper expressively. At the peaks they are hardly eighteen
inches deep, but they have grown at the bottom to five feet,
and they continue to expand, naturally and securely, as they
run off at an angle into the ground (plate 66). It is clear to
anyone where the support for the roof is coming from.

That is all there is to the building externally: a simple,
forthright statement of a geometrical idea. It is as successful
and appropriate as any application of the hyperbolic paraboloids during their popularity. The junction between the low
points and the ground have never been handled better. The
whole roof, which after all is practically the whole building,
grows easily out of the earth, and the water which it collects
spills neatly down between each pair of edge-beams into
drainage pools. The effect of these junctions has been somewhat spoiled at close quarters by the addition of slipshod
and rusty barbed-wire fences round each base, a precau-
tionary afterthought by the authorities to prevent children
from having the bicycle ride of their lives over the saddle.
Furthermore, the roofing has leaked in a few spots and the
brown rings on the ceiling have not been cleaned away. But
one comes to expect administrative untidiness of this sort in
Japanese buildings.

The lack of maintenance plagues most of Tange's work,
since most of it is public work. At Shizuoka it might be said
that the architect, having learned from experience at Hiroshima, accepted the fact that the building would be untidy
in use anyway, and so, in sympathy, made the structure
itself a little untidy. In this building he has achieved an un-
Japanese and uncraftsmanlike roughness which even Le
Corbusier could envy. The fins on the main walls, for example, are not evenly spaced; the big edge-beams twist casu-
ally. These things do not look deliberate, but I do not imagine
that they worried anyone when the forms came away from the
concrete and exposed what had set inside. Somehow the lack

of precision is part of the easy-going public park and is a realistic expression of a low budget and of provincial trades-men inexperienced with concrete. In any event the coarse and irregular construction adds to the power of the building in an inverted way. It stresses that only one thing matters here: one big idea, to be accepted or rejected, an idea that is above concern with trivialities such as accurate measurements.

In a similar way Tange permitted, even welcomed, inter-ruptions to the wall treatments. For instance, the ends of two internal beams which carry the seating gallery poke through the external panels and cling to the nearest external fin for support (plate 62). They offer no apology or explanation for their presence to the viewer from outside, but they do not matter because the building is bold enough to sweep past interruptions.

From the inside, the roof shape is impressive and con-vincing. The seating is arranged around three quarters of the square, leaving the rest for performance (plate 67). Exit doors between all the fins on the approach side promise easy access for the most impatient crowd.

When they were the rage, hyperbolic paraboloids were ex-citing things. Obviously the temperature drops with famili-arity, and the only relevant question is whether what remains looks appropriate. Five years after the event, after all the excitement, Shizuoka passes this test. It sits calmly in its park, its drooping curve seen from the side reversing the curves of the wooded mountain range behind. Yet it is not sound asleep; it still is a commanding presence. In fact, it has just the kind of dynamic balance between extremes that Tange seeks.

The Office and Assembly Buildings for the Kagawa Pre-fectural Government at Takamatsu (plates 69–76), on the island of Shikoku across the Inland Sea, are probably Tange's best-known work after Hiroshima. They mark the climax of his third phase: the trabeated or beam-glorifying phase. The ten-story island administration block which dominates the composition derives its entire character from the effects of isolated, accentuated, crossing, counterpoised beams. It is all reinforced concrete, but at first glimpse it appears to be the biggest timber teahouse in the world.

Many of Tange's admirers consider this building his best. It is an excellent example of his confident work in mid-career. On the other hand, it is possibly the most controversial of all his buildings. The timber look of the structure greatly dis-turbs some of his critics, who see it as an invalid translation of a traditional form into a foreign modern material. The timber effect of the concrete is not only derived from the grain and knots transferred from the wooden formwork, but mainly from the appearance of carpentry technique in the jointing and crossing of the beams, and from the unexpected proportions of many of them: very deep but thin, like wooden planks (plate 74). Unquestionably, the volume of visible concrete could be reduced by half without any fear of the balconies' collapsing. However, it can be argued that reinforced concrete used in this way is a negative form of timber construction, since the formwork into which it is poured is erected by a carpenter. Thus these square-cut beams are as valid as any curious plastic curves, curves which might suit the finished material but not its method of erection.

If you are not impressed with the pros and cons of such ethical arguments, you will probably be content to note that the Kagawa Office justifies its methods visually. It is highly circumspect and faithful within the discipline selected by the architect. It sits in a vigorously conceived garden of water and rugged stones which complements the structure with its sympathetic scale. The artistic unity is never broken in the structure. It is, however, disturbed by minor irrelevant decorative adjuncts, such as the restless penthouse, which contains some little square blocks projecting in a diagonal pattern, and one wall with random perforations in pure Corbu-style.

The Sogetsu Art Center in Tokyo (plates 77–85) was designed and built concurrently with the Kagawa Office, and it has the same carpentry effect in its giant twin beams checked out to grip the thick edges of floor and roof (plate 77). It is much more massive in form, however, and it carries Tange into the beginning of his fourth creative phase, in which beams, windows, and all other smaller elements are subjugated to the massive sculptural whole.

The main bulk of the Sogetsu is raised above a deeply recessed, glazed entrance floor which lies between the forecourt and the rear sculpture garden. Entering from the forecourt, a visitor climbs eight steps which run the full length of the building. These steps, similar to a Greek stylobate, help to detach the open foyer from the busy street. Viewed from the street, Sogetsu presents an almost impervious façade, broken only by a row of glazed windows lost in the shadow of the roof projection, and a row of six little hooded slits on the second-floor level. By sinking the auditorium of the building partially into the ground, Tange has used its roof as the floor of the entrance foyer and as the sculpture garden (plate 82).

The two floors above the foyer house classrooms and offices, and have three solid walls planned as a "U" facing away from the traffic. The fourth wall is glass overlooking the rear courtyard. The exteriors of the blank walls to the street and sides are, unexpectedly, not stripped concrete but have

34 been finished in heavy blue ceramic tile. These have been laid in courses of random width, which provides a liveliness that lightens the gargantuan bulk of the building and its beams. With assistance from such devices, the Sogetsu succeeds in being strong without being gross.

More important, it is a building for the display, teaching, and encouragement of rather *furyu* things like flower arrangement. Without offending *furyu*, it puts it firmly in its place.

The small city of Imabari on the island of Shikoku, facing the Inland Sea, is where Tange spent his boyhood. His work on its City Hall buildings about thirty years later brought closer the fourth and current phase of his creative development.

The group's main elements are an office block and a public auditorium (plates 86–94). They were designed in 1957 and built in 1959. The structures are as massive as Sogetsu, but the carpentry look is gone. Like Shizuoka, they make more of the plastic freedom of concrete. The walls of the office block and Council Chamber are designed as three-dimensional traps for shadows. They zigzag in plan and, on the east and west sides, bold webs and beams span the points of the zigzag to shade the wall surface (plate 94). The long, tall side walls of the public auditorium also are folded, but the folds are out of parallel, so that the surface is divided into triangular planes, the prominent ones wider at the top where they support the uptilted plane of the roof overhang (plate 91). At the ends of the building this uptilted roof overhang grows to enormous proportions (plates 87, 88), sharply recalling Le Corbusier's Ronchamp Chapel.

The Dentsu Office Building in Osaka (plates 95–101) is Tange's most vulgar work. This is appropriate and not surprising, for the Dentsu is a huge advertising agency and the building houses studios for such non-reticent media as television and radio. The surprising thing is that the company had the sophisticated sense to commission a creative architect. This it did in 1957, and the building was completed in 1960.

Osaka is "sometimes called the Venice of the Orient" according to the tourist pamphlets, referring to the canals in its midst. Actually it is the Milan of the Orient, and like Milan it has scores of modern business blocks some ten stories high which are thoroughly respectable and representative examples of mid-century international commercial building, and which would discredit no city in the world. If you stand on one bridge of the Dojima River in the middle of town you can see a dozen clean, capably designed nearcubes with filing-cabinet fronts in metal or concrete, with rather less than the international average complement of

stuck-on lettering, murals, and advertising symbols, and with
much less than the international average content of color. All
is gray, for the national tradition of not painting lingers on in
modern Japan even in the hotbeds of commerce. One of these
buildings is Tange's, the Dentsu.

Immediately, however, the Dentsu stands apart—but not
because of Tange's escapade in vulgarity, which, it need
hardly be stressed, takes a gentlemanly turn. At first glimpse,
vulgar display is limited in fact to two big, coarse sans-serif
words stuck to the penthouses: "Dentsu," in white, and "Advertising," in blue (plate 95). The architecture clearly would
be considerably better without this lettering and it was obviously not the architect's idea. The Dentsu stands apart because its front, which faces the canal, is not just a bland,
closed filing cabinet. It is something with depth and solidity
and evidence of the varying activities which are enclosed. For
instance, Tange has accepted—in fact, obviously he has welcomed—the need for the television and radio studios on two
of the upper floors to be isolated from street noises and natural light. He has broken the even grid with a firm blank panel
across these two floors. Again, he has recessed all the glass of
the façade out of sight of the summer sun, so that a pedes-
trian across the canal is conscious only of a pattern of light-
gray planks of various widths: horizontal ones for floors and
balustrades, and vertical ones for sun baffles. These planks
float against the dark shadows of the hollows. In addition,
Tange has cut a deep recess down each side of the front,
broken only by balconies separating the central grid from the
side walls (plate 100). It must be admitted that the functional
realism of this device is not so apparent.

The planks of the Dentsu façade are precast concrete
blocks of large size. The joints between them are clean-cut
and accentuated, about half an inch wide, recessed, and dark.
They set up a minor pattern against the major one of the solids
and the voids. The two side walls (plate 101) which partially
frame the façade are not crisply rectilinear like the rest but
curve outward. This device also does not explain itself, un-
less one considers curves as an acceptable frame. Curves
appear again in the entrance porch (plate 97), and inside the
foyer where they are reflected in the voluptuously rounded
corners of the concrete beams on the ceiling and in the up-
sweep of a mezzanine balcony. Overhead a circumspect con-
fection of pale yellow plastic tubes and lights sways gently
in the air conditioning.

The visual problem of a highly competitive commercial
office block in a crowded city, with practically nothing but its
front showing to the street, normally reduces itself to a two-
dimensional pattern for a façade, designed like typography.

36 It is not a problem to inspire creative architects, and for this good reason they are seldom given the opportunity to consider it.

The Dentsu is a rare exception and Tange managed the task with remarkable success. He avoided blank anonymity and he avoided any obvious commercialism. He made it a three-dimensional form and he kept it under control. At the same time, in the process he frankly permitted some of the realities of function and structure to be distorted a little in the interest of the realities of advertising.

Kurashiki is a pretty little old city near the Inland Sea about halfway between Osaka and Hiroshima. It is the national center of the *tatami* craft and its population of some 130,000 lives under a compact sea of bronze-tiled roofs. Further out, rows of factory chimneys confirm the guide's information that this area is growing fast.

You drive through the ancient city along winding streets, sometimes with open drains, always so narrow that a car and a bicycle could not possibly pass each other, yet frequently do. Suddenly your taxi is ejected into a wide dusty square, and there before you is the strongest and strangest thing that Tange ever built.

The Kurashiki City Hall (plates 102–111), designed in 1958 and finished in 1960, has been called his masterpiece. Unquestionably it marks the climax of his work to date. It is the first section of a plan to provide a community center for Kurashiki, linking with two fine established art museums nearby and with a festival hall which Tange will build later at one side of an open square to be developed in front of the present building (plate 108).

This first section is essentially an office block, standing free, about one hundred and eighty feet long and three tall stories high. It is not immediately apparent that the block contains three stories, however, because the floor lines are lost behind the wall treatment, which for most of the façade is a series of uneven, narrow horizontal slits between concrete planks of similar width (plates 102, 104). In places the slits reveal recessed balconies, and over the ground-floor entrance, but off center, a balcony projects forward. Thus, instead of the familiar even grid to an office building of this kind, Kurashiki City Hall presents an irregular composition of planks with small square blocks spacing them apart and dark recesses between, all sandwiched between two robust bands of stripped concrete, one at second-floor level and one at the roof. The planks and blocks are sharply cut, as in the Dentsu Building, and the ends of the planks at corners are stacked deliberately out of line to accentuate their separate-

ness (plate 111). Quite seriously, it has the elementary, in-
nocent character of a child's building-block construction.

The glazed wall of the ground floor is recessed. Instead of
a series of columns to support the superstructure, there are
only two huge intermediate supports. The upper floors are
carried between these on long-span concrete beams. This division of the building into three big main structural bays is
immediately apparent, and it is emphasized by an enormous
concrete block on top, which later one discovers to be the wall
of an open-air amphitheater sitting on the roof over the central bay.

The division into three is still emphatic when one enters.
The central bay is an enormous open foyer, the full width
of the building and about thirty feet high—occupying two
full stories and mezzanines. Tange calls this a Citizens' Hall
Lobby. Exhibitions may be shown, and people may meet here.
When I asked how often the huge space is in practice used
for such purposes a city official said wryly, "Trade union
delegations use it." This super-scale lobby is not air conditioned, but the concentrated municipal offices which occupy
the two outside bays of the building are air conditioned, and
are comfortable and conventional in scale. These two matching end bays also carry the service ducts and stair shafts.

This symmetrical arrangement of the building is evident
in the plan drawings (plate 108). None of the arbitrary irregularity of the block-building technique which was seen
on the outside is to be found in a tightly disciplined and beautifully simple order. The various floor plans build up logically to
the top, where the central section is finally occupied by the
Council Chamber, ringed by the mayoral offices and conference rooms. All the small subsidiary offices are very straight-
laced and impeccably designed with a little wood, a touch of
color in upholstery only, and the austere gray background
predominating. It is, therefore, particularly unexpected to
enter the central Council Chamber and to be transported, in
an agreeable and quite amusing way, to another atmosphere
altogether.

The Council Chamber (plate 107) is quite clearly deriva-
tive of Le Corbusier's ovoid period. It glows white from
walls finished in thickly spattered roughcast cement and is
lighted by concealed natural and artificial sources somewhere
at the top. All is curved and cornerless, and overhead hangs
a great saddle finished in similar roughcast, though slightly
grayed, dipping in the middle of the room and rising high
over the mayoral dais at one end and over the public visitors'
gallery at the other. The curves and the rough texture immediately evoke visions of Le Corbusier's Ronchamp Chapel,

38 and yet the atmosphere here is quite different; it is not solemn but spritely.

The sudden impact of this white egg interior is as disarming as it is unexpected. The debt to Le Corbusier is so open and undisguised that one has to accept the room in the spirit of a tribute to the master. But still a puzzle remains. How could an architect of such sensitivity as Tange inject such a foreign and feminine form into the very heart of this uncompromisingly masculine, bony building? How could he design anything so devastating to the artistic unity of the whole? The answer, I suppose, is that he did not. This delightful but irrelevant chamber was probably a separate thing, designed by one of his team during Tange's five months' absence in the United States.

There is no other sign of femininity or compromise in the building. Never did the characteristic massiveness of modern Japanese architecture look more rebellious. It seems like a direct reaction against the more delicate traditions of Japan. And Tange will admit that it is. "Lightness or openness or spaciousness in the physical and psychological meaning cannot satisfy people's energies or desires," he said at the University of Hawaii in 1959. "People want castles where they live in. They want castles where they work in. They want eternal or more durable feeling. They do not want weakness or tentativeness, but this weak and tentative feeling that we have in our tradition sometimes appears in the so-called modern architecture of the world."

In Kurashiki, Tange has indeed created durable feeling, and the huge scale of his public space and of his concrete structure may be taken as a symbol of the might of democracy in the municipal government. Perhaps this is a greater reality than functional or structural reality and so may justify the super-strength that sometimes verges on being musclebound. In search of this greater symbolism, then, let us look again at the main lobby, the "Citizens' Hall." It is the visual core and at the same time the most disturbing element of the building. It is disturbing because it is monumental and compelling, but possibly in the wrong way. Its scale is what Tange, in search of dynamic balance between human and superhuman, has described as the mass-human scale. It is very big. If I were an aggrieved unionist waiting to be heard in that enormous volume I think I would be more impressed by the weight of the establishment than by the generosity of democratic procedure.

One departmental chief told me that the building is indeed a little unsettling to the delegates and clerks who use it. He described its quality, interestingly enough, as Grecian, and explained that this is not a familiar atmosphere for his townspeople. Yet they blame themselves for not appreciating it; they are immensely proud of it. "Well, it is world famous," I remarked. "Of course," he said.

The huge stairway which rises to the mezzanine galleries from the concrete-slab paving of the hall restates the mammoth scale. Its immense balustrade is a formal delight, but both the balustrade and the width of the stairway seem designed for some purpose greater than the reality (plate 106). Does the stairway lead up to some significant democratic forum where citizens and council meet? Nothing like that. It rises only to rows of clerks, busy at their desks. Apparently Tange's intention here is to open the municipal machine democratically to the public. Yet the gesture does seem extravagant —not in terms of yen, for Tange is experienced enough to do these things and still keep costs extraordinarily low—but in terms of the psychological effect on the visitor. It may be that there was no error in judgment here. A Western visitor can hardly know all the conditions that led to Tange's decision, and he must admire the force and consistency in execution. The Citizens' Hall has the power of a ceremonial brass band.

To a warm admirer of Tange's works there is another unsatisfying thing about this Hall: the perhaps trivial matter of the treatment of the great concrete walls on either side, each some thirty feet square. In the Tokyo City Hall and the Kagawa Office, Tange side-stepped the forbidding austerity of his exclusively gray architectural finishes by introducing colorful ceramic murals by other artists. In the Kurashiki building he uses decorative elements of his own contrivance. Not unexpectedly, the walls are of raw, stripped concrete. Less expectedly, they have been scored by shallow arbitrary lines which produce a thin pattern in which recesses have been formed as focal points. Each of these recesses carries a comparatively small panel painted a primary color. These recesses seem to be some sort of windows opening onto the office space behind them. Moreover, they look like windows of a very particular sort, one which is practically a trademark of Le Corbusier's. The sides, or reveals, are splayed, so that quite a small window panel expands to a big incision in the surface of the thick wall. Furthermore, the splays are uneven, so that the window panel is off-center in the incision.

This is a meaningless little mannerism of Le Corbusier's which is acceptable only in his own buildings and in external walls where the exaggerated splays may have justification as weathering. Tange's explanation is that the uneven recesses were constructed for acoustic reasons: the straight parallel sides of plain concrete would have set up disastrous echoes in the hall. A closer inspection reveals that the red, blue, or yellow paint at the back of each recess is indeed applied to perforated plywood, giving token sound-absorption.

While it is undoubtedly true that these uneven recesses are of some value to the acoustics of the hall, this is, unfortunately, not apparent to the simple viewer, who sees only spots of hard color enthroned as gems of abstract art in over-wide frames. It would seem, once again, that someone in the Tange team had been studying Le Corbusier too long and too late at night. It seems a pity that the team did not talk this one out. It is almost inexplicable that any organization capable of such demonstrated creativity in form and proportion, should be so impressed by the old master as to want to use his toys, and to misuse them at that. The overt copying of Le Corbusier's mannerisms in unassimilated details is the only thing left which one could call a mistake in Tange's mature work.

One of the latest of Tange's works, the library at Rikkyo University in the outskirts of Tokyo (plates 112–118), shows him growing more confident and more sensitive. Rikkyo has a collegiate Gothic campus dating from the First World War. As in its Western university prototypes, all is red brick. This is surprising, considering Japan is an earthquake-conscious and almost brickless land. The buildings are pleasantly spaced and attractively interspersed with trees. The old library building had a cathedral ceiling of dark wood and open Gothic-like trusses. Tange's commission in 1959 called on him to add an entirely new library, connected with the old one, in a corner of the university grounds. The building he produced in 1961 demonstrates very clearly three aspects of Tange's design methods at this stage of his development.

First, the practical and professional side: the building plan is a picture of orderliness, as always. The main offices and stacks are contained in a tall rectilinear single-story block. The reading room section, in two stories, sits on top; but it occupies less than half the area of the offices and leaves the rest of the roof clear as a sundeck for outdoor study (plate 113). At the other end of this deck a generous, if not actually gigantic, stairway leads down to the ground where it meets a pathway of the campus (plate 112). Students may use this as their direct approach to the reading room, by way of the sundeck, short-cutting the office area. Everything works in a straightforward, practical, and organized way.

The same can be said of the way Tange tackled the problem of blending a new building into a Gothic-revival community which is forty-five years and a world away from modern Japan. His first concession was to use a similar red brick for his main walls, matching the color of the old campus buildings. Then he kept the main lower block negative enough to

fit anywhere. These two gestures hardly constituted a ceremonial bow, but they were adequately polite under the cir-
cumstances.

The form of the reading room superstructure, however, is
not negative, and has nothing to do with the Gothic. And it
is here that the second element of Tange's design method is apparent. The main wall, facing south onto the sundeck, is entirely glazed, and the top is spanned by the usual massive
roof edge-beam of naked stripped concrete, with the pattern
of narrow wooden boards used in its formwork lending it the
familiar knotty texture (plate 113). But what is unusual here
is that this roof beam, and the roof behind it, are bent. The
beam droops in an arc, following that most characteristic of
all Japanese traditional building shapes. It is the line of the
pagoda eaves, the lintel of the temple gateway, the shrine
roof: a drooping line based somewhere in antiquity on the
deflection of over-stressed roofing logs. It is a sag, but not
a wilting, pessimistic one because its supports are not at the
extremes, but are set in from each end, and the often exaggerated upward tilt of the projecting ends is full of spirit.

On the Rikkyo Library roof Tange resurrects the shape,
yet not cheaply as a historic symbol. It happens that this shape
is also sympathetic to the nature of reinforced concrete. Here
it evokes tradition in an unforced and attractive way; but,
more important, its powerful sweep has the visual effect of a
lid to the building, holding all the other parts together.

In these other parts of the building, especially the smaller
parts, the third element of Tange's present design method
becomes apparent. In shaping the over-all form he creates a
structure of dominating strength. The Rikkyo bent roof is one
example, but when the conditions are more propitious, as at
Shizuoka or Kurashiki, he shapes some all-embracing monolithic form. Then, having established this powerful image, he
settles down to vigorous back-pedaling. He loosens up the stiff
edges of the form and allows himself to introduce one or two
irrelevancies.

This method of design may persist in Tange's future work,
and it allows for much variation and further development.
But while the sense of conviction is already complete in the
basic forms, Tange appears to be still feeling his way to a
personal expression in the minor elements. At Rikkyo he uses
again the device of the off-balance window opening, Corbu-
style, although in this case the openings are at least real
windows. Primary color is also injected violently, De Stijl-
style, in unexpected little patches of vivid yellow in the glass
of the north wall.

It is not especially to the credit of Rikkyo Library, as a
work of architecture, that one can see the three stages of the

design process acting almost separately. Under the difficult conditions of adding to an existing building, however, it is surprising that anything of value was achieved. Clearly the upper reading room, under its evocative sagging roof, looking south over the wide sundeck, is a room of great distinction.

A Plan for Tokyo

Beyond the work of designing for other people's use, or for his own use at home, there is a third, more remote but possibly more revealing, segment of Tange's professional activities. This is his practical dreaming: the idealistic projection of his thinking into schemes for vast city planning and Utopian rebuilding.

Town planning hardly exists in Japan, even in the limited way it is practiced by the traffic-planners of most cities in Western countries. Hiroshima crept back onto the atomic ashes with all but the central part in almost as bad a tangle as before. Elaborate modern buildings are erected in country towns on feudal lanes barely twelve feet wide. However, the pressures of traffic and the inconveniences of dispersal in the biggest city in the world finally have reached public awareness. Even reasonably fortunate workers in Tokyo have to travel for some two hours to and from home. The city's much-publicized night life is practically finished by 9 P.M. simply because everyone but the tourist has to start for the suburbs.

Early in 1961 the Tange team published, in magazines and in a privately circulated book, a scheme entitled: "A Plan for Tokyo, 1960—Toward a Structural Reorganization." It was offered as a basis for some concrete thinking "to the many people who are distressed by Tokyo's present condition." The proposal was well illustrated with photographs of an elaborate model, well reasoned, with charts and statistics. It was well received by the converted, and as solidly opposed as one might expect by the conservatives.

⌐ It is a dramatically bold idea for the decongestion of Tokyo in four five-year plans.⌐ The report begins by accepting the realistic forecast that Tokyo will inevitably get bigger still, and explains that most of the congestion is brought about by the radial structure of the city. A city of ten million or more people can no longer focus on a central hub. The solution is to break this center into a linear extension of linked hubs, "somewhat like the vertebrae in the spine." This forms a wide, long "civic axis" which should start at the present downtown hub of Tokyo and project outward, for as many miles as necessary. But in which direction? It could cut through existing suburbs, or it might reach out to link with a new government center at the foot of Mt. Fuji. Any such schemes would

have great difficulties with land acquisition. So the Tange
team turned its back to the existing suburbs and drew the
civic axis out into Tokyo Bay. Building over the bay would be
more costly, they admitted, but "there would be a minimal
risk of land speculation." Furthermore, Tokyo would once
again become a seaside city. Eventually the elevated highways
on each side of the new civic axis would reach right across
the bay to land on the other shore (plate 119).

The plan showed office and recreation buildings occupying
the "vertebrae," and housing units growing out from each
side, their access roads stemming from the joints between
vertebrae (plate 124). To furnish this beautifully simple
fifty-billion-dollar master plan Tange proposed only two
principal kinds of buildings. For the residential sections
(plates 120–22, 126) he proposed a building type which he
first developed a year earlier in leadership of a student team
at M.I.T. In the over-all form the building is like a gigantic
tent. Residences line the sloping outside walls and communal
facilities occupy the space between. In the M.I.T. scheme the
sloping walls of the tent were straight. In this case they have
been allowed to take on a Japanese droop, and the rhythmic
effect of these enormous curved tents floating over Tokyo Bay
would be reminiscent of the roofs of a Japanese village, en-
larged about a hundred times (plate 122).

The big structures would be fixed and permanent, but it is
Tange's idea to let people plan their own houses on platforms
created in the tent walls. Here he is trying to resolve the conflict between the major structures which modern organization
demands but which restricts individuality, and the minor
structures like houses which should be free and short-lived.
"We have tried," the report explains, "to provide freedom
within a more systematic spatial structure."

The other building type is for the offices in the civic axis
(plates 123–125). Since it is reasonable to want to reduce the
number of foundations when one is building over water,
Tange has devised a series of suspended office blocks. Square
towers carrying elevators and services rise at regular inter-
vals, some two hundred feet apart, and office blocks span
them, cantilevering slightly beyond. The bottom of some
blocks may be a hundred feet or more above the ground, and
they cross each other at different heights. The great span is
achieved by building the side walls of the offices as triangu-
lated trusses. The free flow of space around, between, over,
and under these suspended offices suggests the most delightful
open environment, in contrast, let it be said, to the threat of
a certain amount of dinginess under the residential tents.
This office design is as bold as anything Tange has conceived.
It is full of potential unexpected delights, and difficulties. But

44 Tange has never been timid about facing difficulties. He is working at the time of writing on an actual office building for downtown Tokyo based on the same idea: the offices suspended high above ground between two widely-spaced service shafts. This promises to be even stronger than Kurashiki, with more concentration on the formal, structural image; even bolder, with irrelevancies almost eradicated. It promises to be as big a step forward as Tange has ever taken, and it reminds one that he is hardly yet at the prime of his creative life, and undoubtedly will be taking more steps, as big, but in the same straight line, after this one.

The buildings illustrated in the following pages demonstrate clearly, in a way which the works of few other architects do, a chronological personal development. The Children's Library at Hiroshima (plate 17) and the University Library at Rikkyo (plate 112), for instance, are two comparable buildings from the beginning and the end of the corpus of Tange's work to this stage. They serve similar functions and yet they have at first sight practically nothing in common. They might have been by different hands. But the man who was responsible for both has not, in fact, changed his convictions. These convictions have always given him impressive strength, which has been tempered by his human sensitivity to broader issues. Only the degree of tempering appears to have changed.

At the beginning Tange was an intellectual rather than an emotional artist. He had reasons for everything he did, even if on rare occasions they were clear only to him. Emotions to him have never constituted reasons. Obviously, he would have done nothing, however good the reason, if he had not expected that the appearance would be good, but appearances and emotions were not his motivation. Today, his emotional convictions *ride beside,* and on rare occasions *override,* his logic. There is no telling how soon he will revert to a more rationalized and reasoned approach. His latest projects suggest that even now he is swinging back a little, indicating that he will finally achieve, somewhere between, the balance and the greatness as an architect which his native talent promises.

Tange has some towering qualities as an architect. He has a natural aptitude for handling form and space, and his confidence grows steadily with experience. He is a thinker, an able writer even in the foreign English tongue, a teacher, a leader of thought, a national figure. His work in many ways is a symbol of the new Japan. He is an artist with an objective. This objective is simple. No one could quarrel with it or argue that it is not important. He is searching for the truth,

or as he puts it "the reality," along the tiny segment of total
life that is his artistic orbit. He hopes to find the reality by
balancing out the incompatibles. He will not succeed all along
the line, of course; he is very human. But he will succeed, as
he already has, in finding satisfactory balances between some
of the inconsistencies which face him.

As yet, he has not found the satisfying balance between
those inconsistent sides of his own artistic nature: the social
realist and the creative expressionist. No one knows better,
or will stress more emphatically than he, that this is still his
major and unresolved problem. If now he is more obviously,
even spectacularly, expressing himself as well as his building,
this is perhaps inevitable in the climate of the exhibitionism
now pervading Japanese architecture. Today every yard of
concrete poured under his directions is photographed from a
dozen angles by the Japanese architectural press. Nevertheless, Tange is a perfectionist who never satisfies himself and
who never loses sight of his objective. When asked which of
his buildings pleases him most, he answered, "Always the
one I'm working on next."

Notes to the Text

1. In addition to these more official honors, many well-known Western architects estimate Tange highly. "In my opinion, he is already now a man of world format, with an amazing production in a relatively short time," wrote Walter Gropius in a letter to the author, August, 1961. John E. Burchard, after a visit to Japan early last year, wrote, "If dignity and grace and repose and almost immaculate design are the hallmarks of one kind of great architect (and I think they are), then the works of Kenzo Tange have been telling us ever since Hiroshima that he is a great architect" (from the *Architectural Record*, April, 1961, pp. 134–136). Lawrence B. Anderson recalls his presence at M.I.T. as "a vital creative force, independent and strong." Henry Seckel of Hawaii considers that Tange's greatest achievement is "giving appropriate form to the new Japan without diluting the essence of her heritage" (from a letter to the author of November, 1961).

2. His major work so far is *Katsura: Tradition and Creation in Japanese Architecture*, Yale University Press, 1960. This book was suggested by Walter Gropius on a visit to Japan in 1954 and includes an introduction by him. In addition to this introduction and the Tange text, *Katsura* consists mainly of Yasuhiro Ishimoto's fine photographs of the 17th-century palace. These were taken in consultation with Tange.

3. In January, 1960, the popular magazine *Bungei Shunju* (which has been described as the *Saturday Evening Post* of Japan) took a small sampling of cultivated opinion—architects, artists, critics, and so on—and, after tabulation, presented a sort of hit-parade rating of the ten best architects now at work in Japan. In this list, Mayekawa was first and Tange third. One might have expected a different result: that the subtleties of Tange's quieter approach might be missed by the public but would be applauded by the experts. Instead, it seems that Mayekawa's spectacular work excites the intellectuals and scares the public.

4. Speech at the World Design Conference, Toyko, May, 1960.

5. On participating in the new CIAM talks of September, 1959.

6. Speech at the World Design Conference, *op. cit.*

7. CIAM talk, *op. cit.*

8. Speech at the World Design Conference, *op. cit.*

9. Wright's Imperial Hotel, built in time to remain standing proudly through the 1923 earthquake, was in his most personal, ornamental, bravura style, and seemed to have no general lesson for Japan. Its fascinating patterns of space between restrictive galleries and generous foyers stimulated the younger Japanese architects, but Wright's work in Japan remained somehow exotic and foreign.

1. *Peace Memorial Museum, Hiroshima, 1949–56. Southeast corner seen from Community Center Building.*

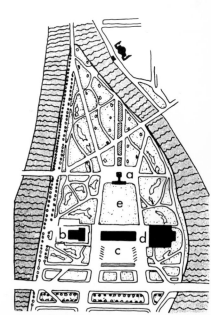

2. *Site plan of Peace Park and related buildings, Hiroshima:*
a. Memorial; b. Auditorium and Hotel; c. Museum; d. Community Center Building;

3. *Peace Memorial Museum, Hiroshima. Entry stairway from the south.*

4. *Museum. Exterior, south façade.*

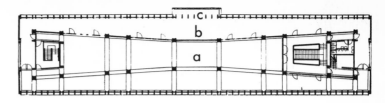

5. *Peace Memorial Museum. Floor plan:*
   a. exhibition hall; b. terrace; c. balcony.

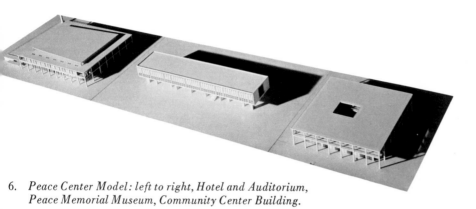

6. *Peace Center Model: left to right, Hotel and Auditorium,*
   Peace Memorial Museum, Community Center Building.

7. *Memorial to the Dead, Hiroshima. (Community Center Building at left, Peace Memorial Museum at rear.)*

8. *Community Center Building. East façade.*

9. *Community Center Building. Southeast corner.*

10. *Community Center Building. Interior, central court.*

11. *Community Center Building. Plans: A. Ground floor. B. Second floor. C. Third floor.*

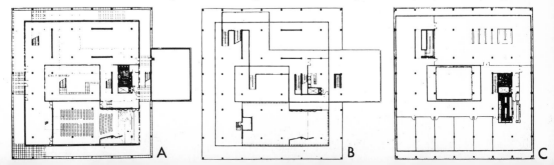

A   B   C

12.   *Ehime Convention Center, Matsuyama, 1952–53. Aerial view.*

13.   *Ehime. Detail of exterior, concrete piers supporting sloped auditorium floor.*

14. *Ehime. View of all units (small hall with trumpet construction is at right).*

15. *Ehime. View of interior.*

16. *Ehime. Exterior of small hall connecting with administration offices and large hall at the right.*

17.　*Children's Library, Hiroshima, 1951–52. Night view of exterior.*

18.　*Children's Library. Interior, view from center*
　　toward exterior.

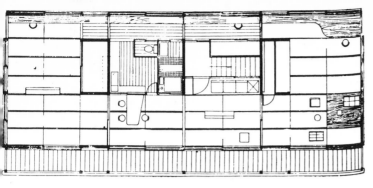

19.   *Tange Residence, Tokyo, 1951–53. Floor plan.*

20.   *Tange Residence. View from the lawn.*

21.   *Tange Residence. Aerial view of roof and site.*

22.   *Tange Residence. Covered patio under living area.*

24. *Tange Residence. Interior view
with painted fusuma.*

25. *Tange Residence. Corner detail of balcony
and roof overhang.*

26. *Tange Residence. Interior.*

27.   *Tange Residence. Interior open onto balcony.*

28. *Tsuda College Library, Tokyo, 1953–54. Entrance façade.*

29. *Tsuda. Reading tables and exterior landscape.*

30. *Tsuda. Reading room with stairway to mezzanine.*

31. *Tsuda. Interior of mezzanine.*

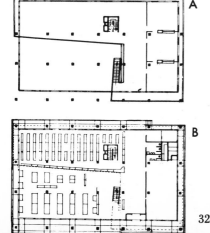

32. *Tsuda. Plans: A. Mezzanine floor.*
B. Ground floor.

33. *Shimizu City Hall, Shizuoka Prefecture, 1953–54. Interior patio.*

34. *Shimizu. Plans: A. Ground floor. B. Second floor (mezzanine). C. Fourth floor. D. Fifth floor (with Council Chamber). E. Roof*

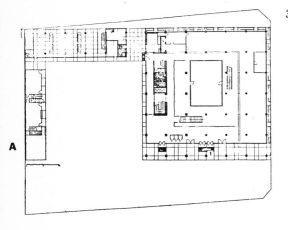

A

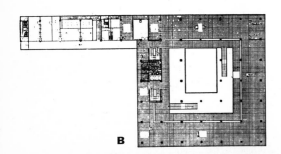

B

C

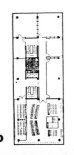

D

E

35.   Shimizu. Interior, entry foyer looking toward interior patio.

36.   Shimizu. Exterior.

37.   *Toshoinsatsu Printing Plant, Numazu, 1953–54. Night view of façade.*

38.   *Toshoinsatsu. Main façade.*

39.   *Kurayoshi City Hall. Detail of platform.*

40.   *Kurayoshi City Hall, Tottori Prefecture, 1955–56. Main entrance, west façade.*

41. *Kurayoshi City Hall. Night view.*

42. *Kurayoshi. Ground-floor entrance.*

43. *Kurayoshi. Exterior, south façade.*

44.   *Kurayoshi. Mezzanine terrace.*

45.   *Kurayoshi. Plan of mezzanine: a. upper part of Assembly Hall;*
      b. upper part of patio; c. upper part of entry; d. offices.

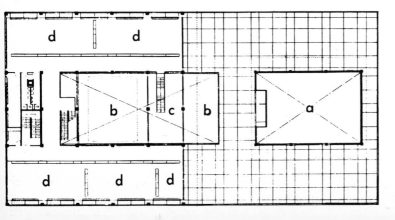

46. *Sumi Memorial Hall. Detail of façade, northeast corner.*

47. *Sumi Memorial Hall, Ichinomiya, 1955–57. East façade with carport entrance.*

48. *Sumi. Foyer opening into Assembly Hall.*

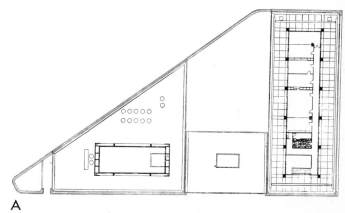

A

49. *Sumi. Plans: A. Second floor. B. Ground floor.*

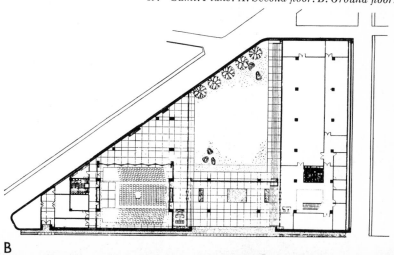

B

50.   *Sumi Memorial Hall. View of entrance and carport.*

51.   *Sumi. Façade of administration building and garden.*

52.   *Tokyo City Hall, Tokyo, 1952–57. Entrance stairway and detail of façade.*

53. *Tokyo City Hall. Staircase in main foyer.*

54. *Tokyo City Hall. Exterior detail showing floodlight.*

55. *Tokyo City Hall. Model of complete
     project, with City Hall (already
     built) in the foreground.*

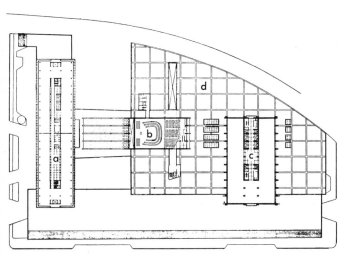

56. *Tokyo City Hall. Plan of model:
     a. non-public offices; b. Council Hall;
     c. public administration offices; d. garden terrace (over parking and lower level facilities).*

57. *Tokyo City Hall. Entrance façade.*

58. *Tokyo City Hall. View into foyer with a mural by Taro Okamoto at right.*

59. *Tokyo City Hall. Interior of auditorium.*

60. *Tokyo City Hall. Office interior (furnishings designed by Mme. Charlotte Perriand).*

61. *Shizuoka Convention Hall, 1955–57. Exterior, view of finned wall with access doors and glazed panels.*

62. *Shizuoka Convention Hall. Detail of blind wall.*

63. *Shizuoka. Cross section.*

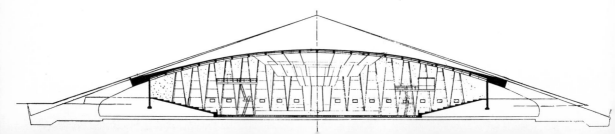

64.   *Shizuoka. Aerial view of exterior.*

65.   *Shizuoka. Plans: A. Balcony. B. Main floor.*

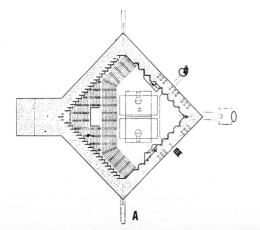
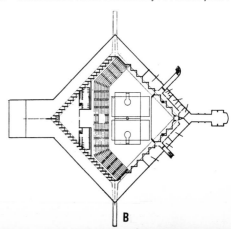

A   B

66. *Shizuoka Convention Hall. Exterior showing low-point, ground-roof juncture.*

67. *Shizuoka. Interior of auditorium seen from stage.*

68. *Shizuoka. Detail of corner, east façade.*

69.   *Kagawa Prefectural Government Office, Takamatsu, 1955–58. Exterior seen from balcony of Assembly Building.*

70. *Kagawa Prefectural Government Office.*
Interior, conference room.

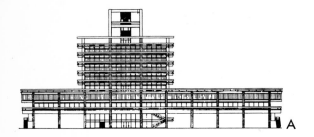

71. *Kagawa. A. East elevation. B. Ground floor. C. Second floor. D. Third floor. E. An office floor. F. Roof and penthouse.*

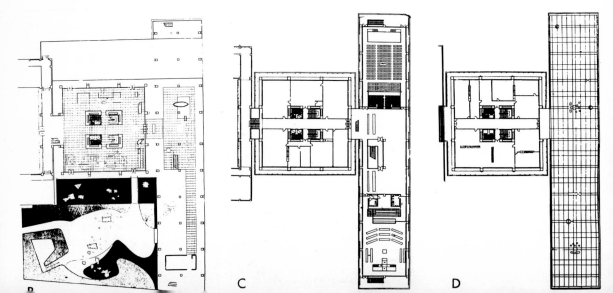

72. *Kagawa. View of garden and Office Building from pilotis of Assembly Building.*

73. *Kagawa. Night view across garden into entry hall. (Ceramic mural by Guen Inokuma.)*

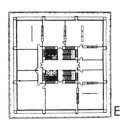

E

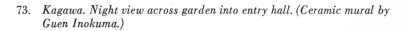

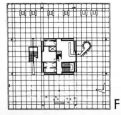

F

74. *Kagawa Prefectural Government Office. Corner structure of Office Building seen from Assembly Building roof.*

75. *Kagawa. Façade of Assembly Building.*

77. *Sogetsu Art Center, Tokyo, 1955–58. Entrance façade.*

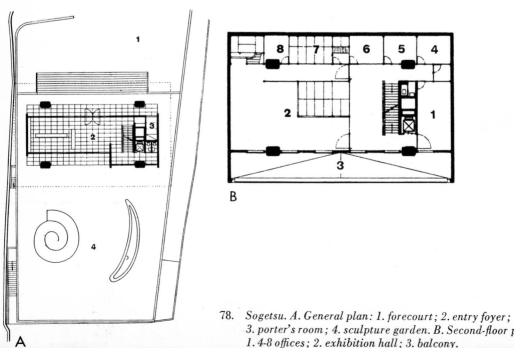

78. *Sogetsu. A. General plan: 1. forecourt; 2. entry foyer;*
3. porter's room; 4. sculpture garden. B. Second-floor plan:
1. 4-8 offices; 2. exhibition hall; 3. balcony.

80. *Sogetsu Art Center. Garden façade.*

81.   *Sogetsu. Penthouse and roof terrace.*

82.   *Sogetsu. Garden (over auditorium roof).*

83. *Sogetsu Art Center. Interior, showing central stairway.*

84. *Sogetsu. Interior of clubroom opening onto garden balcony (table designed by Mme. Charlotte Perriand;* haniwa *displayed at rear).*

85. *Sogetsu. Auditorium foyer, basement level.*

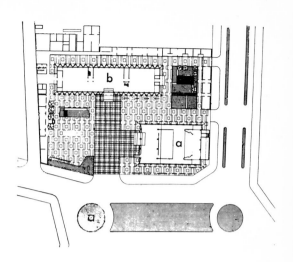

86. *Imabari City Hall, Ehime Prefecture, 1957–59. General plan: a. auditorium; b. municipal offices.*

87. *Imabari. Exterior, with auditorium at left, municipal office building at right.*

88.　*Imabari City Hall. Entrance façade of auditorium.*

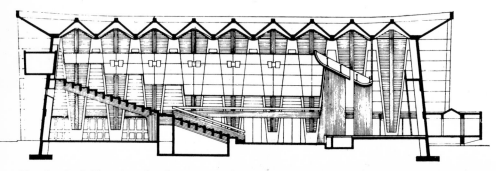

89.　*Imabari. Elevation of auditorium façade.*

90. *Imabari. Detail of auditorium exterior.*

91. *Imabari. Detail of auditorium, looking toward municipal office building.*

92. *Imabari City Hall. Interior of Council Chamber inside municipal office building.*

93. *Imabari. Façade of municipal office building.*

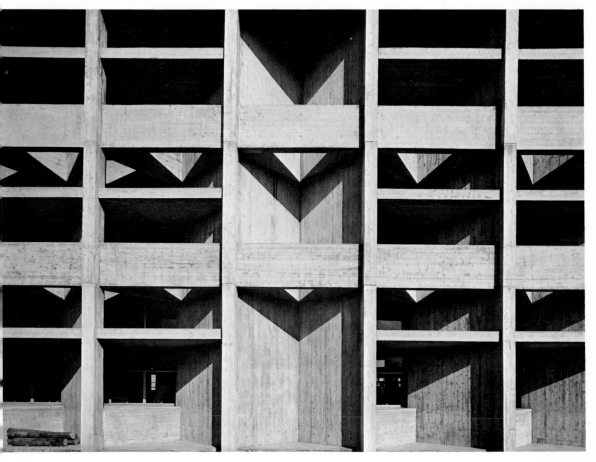

94.   *Imabari. Detail of municipal office building façade.*

95. *Dentsu Office Building, Osaka, 1957–60. Exterior.*

96. *Dentsu. Plans: A. Ground floor. B. Second floor. C. Longitudinal section.*

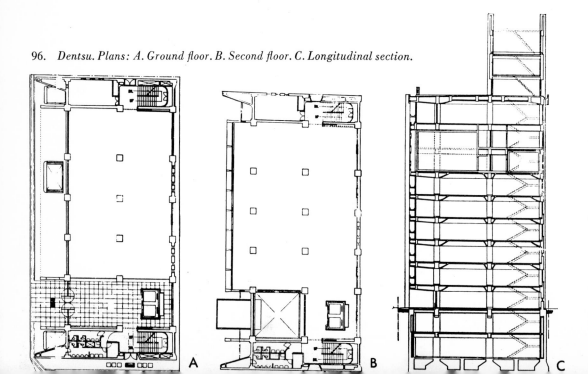

97. *Dentsu. Night view of entrance.*

98. *Dentsu. Interior of an office.*

99. *Dentsu Office Building. Interior of an insulated studio.*

100. *Dentsu. Detail of corner.*

101. *Dentsu. Detail of side wall.*

102. *Kurashiki City Hall, Okayama Prefecture, 1958–60. Façade facing plaza.*

103. *Kurashiki. A. Longitudinal section. B. Main floor. C. Third floor. D. Roof and penthouse.*

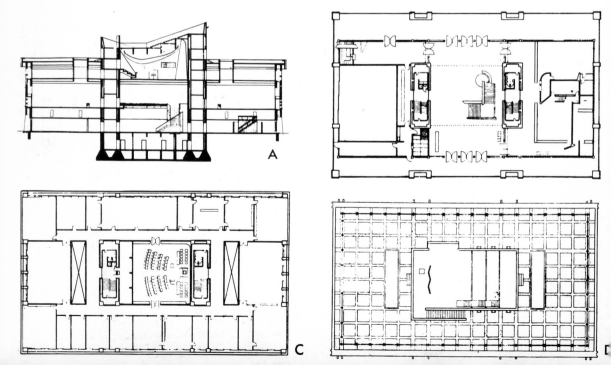

104. *Kurashiki. Rear façade facing street.*

105. *Kurashiki. Aerial view.*

106.   *Kurashiki City Hall. Main stairway in entrance hall.*

107. *Kurashiki. Interior of Council Chamber.*

108. *Kurashiki. Aerial view of model.*

109. *Kurashiki City Hall. Mezzanine view across entrance hall and stairway.*

110. *Kurashiki. Stairway from roof amphitheater.*

111. *Kurashiki. Exterior, corner detail.*

113. *Rikkyo University Library. Sundeck, view toward reading room superstructure.*

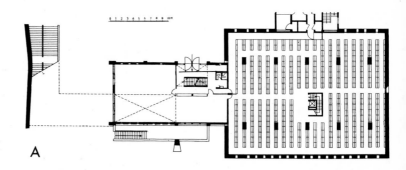

A

114. *Rikkyo Library. Plans: A. Ground floor. B. Lower reading room and sundeck. C. Upper reading room.*

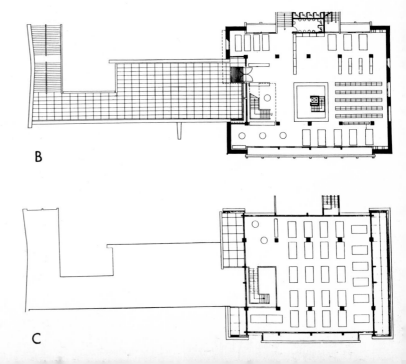

B

C

115. *Rikkyo Library. Student entrance stairway, lower reading room.*

116. *Rikkyo Library. Exterior detail of east façade.*

117. *Rikkyo University Library. View from library office entrance.*

118. *Rikkyo Library. Corner detail.*

119. *A Plan for Tokyo, project, 1960. Units extending across Tokyo Bay.*

120. *Plan of residential buildings: a. residential space; b. public facilities; c. play area;
d. school; e. shopping area; f. car-park; g. railroad station.*

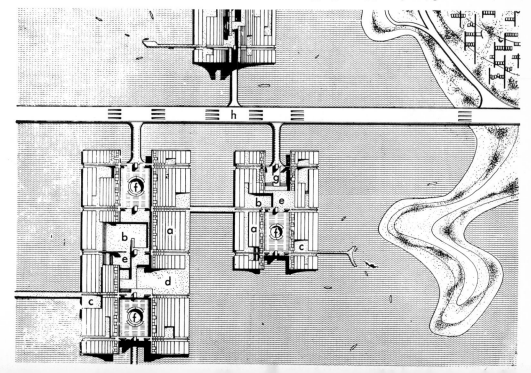

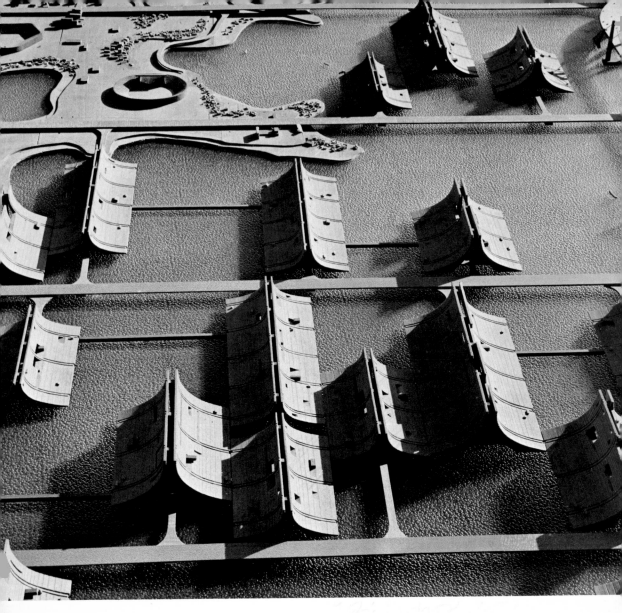

121.   *A Plan for Tokyo. Aerial view of model for residential area.*

123. *Detail of model showing axial transportation system and office buildings suspended between service towers.*

124. *Model of Tokyo axial complex arrangement.*

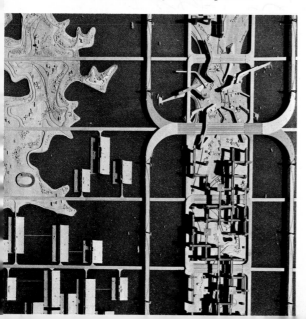

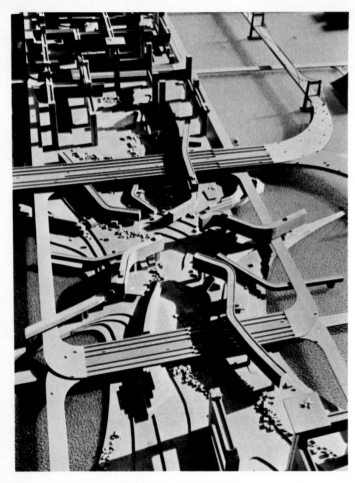

125. *A Plan for Tokyo. Model of suspended office buildings.*

126. *M.I.T. early project for residential units.*

Creation in Present-day Architecture and the Japanese Tradition

by Kenzo Tange

Architectural creation is a special form of comprehending reality. It works upon and transforms reality through the construction of a substantial object of use. The artistic form of this object, on the other hand, has the two-fold quality of both mirroring and enriching reality. This understanding of reality which takes place through architectural creation requires that the anatomy of reality, its substantial and spiritual structure, be grasped as a whole . . .

The realities of present-day Japan, while part of an historically conditioned world-wide reality, are at the same time given their unique shape by the traditions of Japan. Living within this reality, yet also trying always to comprehend it afresh in a forward-looking spirit, these traditions force themselves insistently upon our attention. Were it otherwise, were the problems of today not so pressing, we might accept tradition calmly and unreflectingly as inherited custom, or something out of the past. Only those who adopt a forward-looking attitude realize that tradition exists and is alive. It is therefore only they who can confront and overcome it. This means neither elaborating grandiose schemes for the future nor being fatefully involved with the past, but awareness that the most vital task of today is creatively to elevate both past and future.

Comprehension of reality is reflected in us as thought, as a view of life. Naturally this includes a political aspect and architecture always mirrors the political issues of a society and in turn raises fresh ones. No one would deny that the housing problem or the city problem have political implications. Nevertheless, to be politically active is not the solution for the architect. The proper position for him is to be architecturally active, to try to reflect and mould the realities of society through architectural creation, to grasp reality within architecture. Although reality is outside us it is reflected within us. This inner reality takes shape through the method of architectural creation. Comprehension of reality in architecture occurs through this architectural method and it is in turn deepened by the latter's improvement and enrichment. We contemplate and mould outer reality through the image which has been shaped by the method of architectural creation, through inner reality. Only then and thereby can we come close to the world outside us, and this contact with outer reality in turn changes and enriches the method of into designing a "Japonica" style echoing the interest abroad. In the attitude towards creation represented by stereotyped modernism and its queer offspring, the "Japonica" style, there lurk the traditional moods from *mono-no-aware* to *sabi*. There is a pronounced element of decadence in all this. Such modernism has been accepted most favorably in the sphere of speculative and commercial construction in present Japan . . .

We must, however, not altogether give up hope for a wholesome and progressive development in Japanese contemporary architecture, simply because it has on one side been decaying towards stereotyped modernism and, on the other, adhered to fatalistic realism . . . We can overcome fatalistic realism by comprehending the historical role and achievements of people working in and against this reality and developing it. By so doing we can eliminate from our attitude towards creation and its expression the *mono-no-aware* type of fatalism running through our tradition and can discover a position of sound and progressive realism . . .

Methods of creation in modernistic and functional architecture, putting the cart before the horse, have tried to impose a pattern upon existence through composing in terms of space deduced from a particular way of life or phenomenon of reality. Criticism has often been made by people living and working in these buildings that this restricts their life and I believe their complaints are worthy of attention.

In contrast to such architecture, the traditional houses of the ordinary people, both in Japan and in Western Europe, stand side by side, sharing a similar spatial structure; yet the people inhabiting them do not feel as confined, but manage to use and live in them easily. Here the individual is master, and architecture serves the needs of the inhabitants. In most cases these ordinary houses have been created by people with a positive attitude towards life and an inherent wisdom. The result has been what we might call typification of space and form. The house-type so produced both reflects and gives shape to the development and diversity of real life . . .

The various manifestations of function in the flux and diversity of reality are not beautiful in themselves. Manifestation of function raised to the level of typification—in other words, essential and progressive function—holds the possibility of embodying beauty in expression.

Therefore, typified functions in each historical stage have the possibility of being in accord with the ideal of beauty of the time. To visualize how typified function should be unified with the ideal of beauty represents creation in architecture. This method of approach is also the road to typification.

Only through a positive attitude of grappling with the

poverty of Japan, in other words, through denying our traditional attitudes and further boldly promoting technique is
it possible for us to advance along this road towards typification . . .

In order to achieve typification of space in present-day
architecture, such technical methods as the spanning of wide
spaces and the acquisition of free space through use of such
methods as the utility core, etc., must be further promoted and
developed. Only with such a constructive attitude can the
transient and feeble expression, inherent in our tradition
which has not infrequently led to decadence, be overcome,
and a sounder expression achieved in its place . . .

Our contemporary problems are not always related to tradition, but lie rather in the reality in which we live. An
attitude that fails to realize that tradition is within our inner
selves or simply refuses to face the fact of tradition, does not
result either in the negation or overcoming of tradition in a
true sense.

We can conclude therefore that tradition must first be
recognized and acknowledged. We then become aware that
the expression of some of our architectural works has been
influenced by the traditional passive attitude and we begin
to see the need of taking a positive stand to overcome it . . .
The development of methods in contemporary architecture
is not a mere handing down of traditional methods, but can
be promoted only by bringing architecture face to face with
today's reality.

Biographical Chronology

1913	Born September 4, at Imabari, Ehime Prefecture, Japan
1935–38	Studied at Department of Architecture, Tokyo University
1938	Tatsuno Prize for Graduation, Tokyo University
1942–45	Graduate Course of Architecture, Tokyo University
1946	Professor of Architecture, Tokyo University
1949	Won open competition, Hiroshima Peace Museum project
1951	Member of the International Congresses of Modern Architecture (C.I.A.M.)
1952	Won invited competition, Tokyo City Hall project
1954	Annual Prize of Architectural Institute of Japan
1955	Annual Prize of Architectural Institute of Japan
1957	Jury for Architectural Awards, Bienale, São Paulo
1958	Annual Prize of Architectural Institute of Japan
1958	Pan Pacific Citation of the Hawaiian Chapter of the American Institute of Architects
1959	Prix Internationale d'Art et d'Architecture de *L'Architecture d'Aujourd'hui*, Paris
1959	Ph.D. Degree from Tokyo University. Theme of diploma, "Structure of Tokyo City"
1959	Member of New C.I.A.M.
1959–60	Visiting Professor at Massachusetts Institute of Technology, Cambridge, Massachusetts
1960	Program Chairman, World Design Conference, Tokyo Published *Katsura: Tradition and Creation in Japanese Architecture*
1961	Published *A Plan for Tokyo*
1962	Published *Ise: Origin of Japanese Architecture* (Now printing)
1962	Honorary Doctor of Fine Arts from University of Buffalo

Chronology of Buildings

	DESIGNED	COMPLETED
Hiroshima Peace Hall Project, Hiroshima	1949	1956
Children's Library, Hiroshima	1951	1952
Tange Residence, Tokyo	1951	1953
Ehime Convention Center, Matsuyama (Ehime Prefecture)	1952	1953
Tokyo City Hall, Tokyo	1952	1957
Shimizu City Hall, Shimizu (Shizuoka Prefecture)	1953	1954
Tsuda College Library, Tokyo	1953	1954
Toshoinsatsu Printing Plant, Numazu (Shizuoka Prefecture)	1953	1954
Kurayoshi City Hall, Kurayoshi (Tottori Prefecture)	1955	1956
Shizuoka Convention Hall, Shizuoka	1955	1957
Sumi Memorial Hall, Ichinomiya (Gifu Prefecture)	1955	1957
Kagawa Prefectural Government Office, Takamatsu (Kagawa Prefecture)	1955	1958
Sogetsu Art Center, Tokyo	1955	1958
Imabari City Hall, Imabari (Ehime Prefecture)	1957	1959
Dentsu Office Building, Osaka	1957	1960
Kurashiki City Hall, Kurashiki (Okayama Prefecture)	1958	1960
Rikkyo University Library, Tokyo	1959	1961
Housing Project, Takamatsu (Kagawa Prefecture)	1959	(partially completed)
Office building on two posts, Tokyo	1961	—
Main covered stadium for 1964 Olympics, Tokyo	1961	—

Bibliography

Writings about Kenzo Tange

Articles:

Moffett, Noel, "Kenzo Tange," *Architectural Design*, April, 1958, pp. 151–154.

"Kenzo Tange," *L'Architecture d'Aujourd'hui*, June–July, 1958, pp. 69–77.

"A Japanese Architect Seeks a New Expression," *Architectural Record*, July, 1958, pp. 127–138.

Terry, Charles S., "Kenzo Tange," *Japan Quarterly*, April, 1959, pp. 201–210.

Bourne, R., "Renaissance in Japan," *Architectural Forum*, September, 1959, pp. 96–99.

"New Japanese Architect," *Time* magazine, November 30, 1959, pp. 78–81.

Kollandarud, Guilik, "Kenzo Tange," *Byggekunst* (Norshe Arketecters Landsforbund), No. 2, 1959, pp. 50–56.

Kawazoe, Norboru, "Modern Japanese Architecture Confronts Functionalism," *Zodiac*, III, 1959, pp. 117–148.

Kultermann, Udo, "Kenzo Tange," *Bauen + Wohnen*, January, 1960, pp. 2–30, pp. 1.1–1.16.

"Works of Kenzo Tange," *Annual of Architecture, Structure and Town-Planning*, January, 1960, pp. 25–32.

Kultermann, Udo, "Kenzo Tange," *Das Kunstwerk*, November–December, 1960, pp. 39–50.

"Neues Bauen in Japan," *Form 12*, 1960, pp. 12–13.

Thiel, Philip, "Kurashiki Town Hall by Tange," *Architectural Review*, January, 1961, pp. 3–4.

Smithson, Peter, "The Rebirth of Japanese Architecture," *Architectural Design*, February, 1961, pp. 55–72.

Burchard, John E., "New Currents in Japanese Architecture—Kenzo Tange," *Architectural Record*, April, 1961, pp. 134–37.

"C.I.A.M. Otterlo 1959," *Architectural Design*, May, 1961, pp. 201–202.

"P/A Talks with Kenzo Tange," *Progressive Architecture*, March, 1962, p. 79.

Books:

Kultermann, Udo, *Baukunst der Gegenwast*, Tübingen, Verlag Ernst Wasmuth, 1958, pp. 47–49, 232–236.

———, *Neues Bauen in Japan*, Tübingen, Verlag Ernst Wasmuth, 1958, pp. 35–36. Photos: 1–15, 26–33, 44–51, 72–79, 88–91, 124–127, 156–159.

Articles:

"Creation in Present-Day Architecture and the Japanese Architectural Tradition," *Shinkenchiku* (now *The Japan Architect*), June, 1956, pp. 25–33.

"The Architect in Japan—His Outer World and His Inner World," *Shinkenchiku* (now *The Japan Architect*), October, 1956, pp. 7–13.

"A Central Core for the Tokyo City," *Shinkenchiku* (now *The Japan Architect*), June, 1958, pp. 6–26.

"Architecture and Urbanism": "Aestheticism and Vitalism," pp. 8–10; "Technology and Humanity," pp. 11–12; "A Building and a Project," pp. 13–16, *The Japan Architect*, October, 1960.

"Kenzo Tange, Tokyo, Japan," in Newman, Oscar, ed., *C.I.A.M. 1959 in Otterlo*, Documents of Modern Architecture I, Karl Krämer Verlag, Stüttgart, 1961, pp. 170–185. (Article includes speeches made by Tange at the conference.)

"Architecture and City," *Contemporary Architecture of the World, 1961*, Tokyo, Shokokusha Publishing Co., October, 1961, pp. 86–100.

Books:

With Walter Gropius and Yasuhiro Ishimoto, *Katsura—Tradition and Creation in Japanese Architecture*, New Haven, Yale University Press, 1960; Tokyo, Zokeisha Publishing Co., 1960.

A Plan for Tokyo, 1960, Tokyo, Kenzo Tange Team, March, 1961.

With Norboru Kawazoe and Yoshio Watanabe, *Ise—Origin of Japanese Architecture*, Tokyo, Asahi Newspaper Press, 1962.

Index

Numbers in regular roman type refer to text pages; *italic* figures refer to the plates.

Illustration Credits

L'Architecture d'Aujourd'hui, May, 1956: 19, 32, 34, February 1959: 56, September 1960: 86, 89, October–November, 1961: 96, 103

Bauen und Wohnen, January, 1960: 2, 5, 11, 45, 49, 63, 65, 71, 78

Futagawa, Y., Tokyo: 73, 105, 112, 115, 117

Hirayama, Chuji, Tokyo: 6, 12, 13, 14, 15, 16, 17, 18, 20, 25, 28, 29, 30, 31, 33, 37, 38, 58, 60, 72, 90, 92, 94, 102, 111

Ishimoto, Yasuhiro, Fujisawashi, Kanagawa-Ken, Japan: 1, 3, 4, 7, 9, 10, 22, 23, 27, 46, 51, 69, 70, 75, 76

Kawasumi, Akio, Tokyo: 81, 82, 83, 85, 113, 116, 118, 119, 123, 124, 125, 126

Lubasz, George, New York: Frontispiece

Murai, Shyu, Tokyo: 24

Murasawa, Fumio, Tokyo: 8, 26, 35, 36, 39, 41, 42, 43, 44, 47, 48, 50, 52, 53, 55, 57, 59, 61, 62, 68, 74, 77, 79, 80, 84, 104

Rikkyo University Library, 1960: 114

Taira, Masao, Osaka, Japan: 40, 87, 88, 91, 93, 95, 98, 99, 100, 101, 106, 110

Tange, Kenzo, Tokyo: 21, 54

Tange, Kenzo, *A Plan for Tokyo, 1960* (Tokyo, 1961): 120

Torihata, Eitaro, Tokyo: 64, 66, 67, 108, 121, 122

Tsunenari, S., Osakashi, Japan: 97, 107